PARENTING
NOT JUST A STROLL IN THE PARK

Seven Stages of Family Life

General Editor
LYMAN COLEMAN

Managing Editor
DENISE BELTZNER

Assistant Editors
DOUGLAS LABUDDE
KEITH MADSEN
STEPHEN SHEELY

Cover Art
CHRISTOPHER WERNER

Cover Design
ERIKA TIEPEL

Layout Production
FRONTLINE GROUP

Serendipity House/Box 1012/Littleton, CO 80160   1-800-525-9563

© 1994 Serendipity House. All Rights Reserved.

95 96 97 98 99 /CH/ 6 5 4 3 2 1

ACKNOWLEDGMENTS

To Zondervan Bible Publishers
for permission to use
the NIV text,
The Holy Bible, New International Version
©1973, 1978, 1984 by International Bible Society.
Used by permission of Zondervan Bible Publishers

Instructions for Group Leader

PURPOSE: **What is this course all about?** This course allows you to deal with parenting issues in your life in a supporting group relationship.

SEEKERS/ STRUGGLERS: **Who is this course designed for?** Two kinds of people: (a) Seekers who do not know where they are with God but are open to finding out, and (b) Strugglers who are committed to Jesus Christ, but want to grow in their faith.

NEW PEOPLE: **Does this mean I can invite my non-church friends?** Absolutely. In fact, this would be a good place for people on their way back to God to start.

STUDY: **What are we going to study?** Seven stages of family life (see inside front cover) and Biblical strategies for dealing with them.

FIRST SESSION: **What do we do at the meetings?** In the first session, you get acquainted and decide on the Ground Rules for your group. In sessions two through seven, you have two options for Bible study.

TWO OPTIONS: **What are the two options?** OPTION ONE—This study is best for newly-formed groups or groups that are unfamiliar with small group Bible study. This option primarily contains multiple-choice questions, with no "right or wrong" answers.

OPTION TWO—This study is best for groups who have had previous small group Bible studies and want to dig deeper into the Scriptures. Option Two questions are deeper—and the Scripture is a teaching passage.

CHOOSING AN OPTION: **Which option of Bible study do you recommend?** The OPTION ONE study is best for newly-formed groups, groups that are unfamiliar with small group Bible study, or groups that are only meeting for an hour. The OPTION TWO study is best for deeper Bible study groups, or groups which meet for more than an hour.

CHOOSING BOTH OPTIONS: **Can we choose both options?** If your group meets for 90 to 120 minutes, you can choose to do both studies at the same time. Or you can spend two weeks on a unit—OPTION ONE the first week and OPTION TWO the next. Or you can do one of the options in the meeting and the other option for homework.

SMALL GROUP: **What is different about this course?** It is written for a small group to do together.

GROUP BUILDING: **What is the purpose behind your approach to Bible study?** To give everyone a chance to share their own "spiritual story," and to bond as a group. This is often referred to as "koinonia."

KOINONIA: **What is koinonia and why is it a part of these studies?** Koinonia means "fellowship." It is an important part of these sessions, because as a group gets to know one another, they are more willing to share their needs and care for one another.

BIBLE KNOWLEDGE: **What if I don't know much about the Bible?** No problem. Option One is based on a Bible story that stands on its own—to discuss as though you were hearing it for the first time. Option Two comes with Comments —to keep you up to speed.

COMMENTS: **What is the purpose of the Comments?** To help you understand the context of the Bible passage.

LEADERSHIP: **Who leads the meetings?** Ideally, there should be three people: (a) trained leader, (b) apprentice or co-leader, and (c) host. Having an apprentice-in-training in the group, you have a built-in system for multiplying the group if it gets too large. In fact, this is one of the goals of the group—to give "birth" to a new group in time.

RULES: **What are the ground rules for the group?**

    PRIORITY: While you are in the course, you give the group meetings priority.

    PARTICIPATION: Everyone participates and no one dominates.

    RESPECT: Everyone is given the right to their own opinion, and "dumb questions" are encouraged and respected.

    CONFIDENTIALITY: Anything that is said in the meeting is never repeated outside the meeting.

    EMPTY CHAIR: The group stays open to new people at every meeting as long as they understand the ground rules.

    SUPPORT: Permission is given to call upon each other in time of need at any time.

    CONTINUING: What happens to the group after finishing this course? The group is free to disband or continue to another course. (See pages 63–64 for making a Covenant and continuing together as a group.)

FOUR THINGS YOU NEED TO KNOW ABOUT

Beginning a Small Group

1. PURPOSE: This course is designed for ongoing and special interest groups. The goal is to get better acquainted and become a support group. Using the analogy of a baseball diamond, the goal of a group is home plate or "bonding." To get to home plate, the group needs to go around three bases:

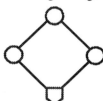

FIRST BASE: History Giving—telling your "story" to one another—your childhood, your journey, your hopes and dreams. SECOND BASE: Affirmation—responding to each other's story with appreciation. THIRD BASE: Need Sharing—going deeper in your story—your present struggles, roadblocks, anxieties, and where you need help from God and the group.

---

2. AGENDA: There are three parts to every group meeting:

GATHERING / 10 min.	**BIBLE STUDY** / 30 min.	**CARING** / 20 min.
Purpose: To break the ice and become better acquainted	Purpose: To share your spiritual journey	Purpose: To share prayer requests and pray

---

3. FEARLESS FOURSOME: If you have more than seven in your group at any time, call the option play when the time comes for Bible Study, and subdivide into groups of four for greater participation. (In four's, everyone will share and you can finish the Bible Study in 30 minutes.) Then regather the group for the Caring Time.

GATHERING	**BIBLE STUDY**	**CARING**
All Together	Groups of 4	Back Together

---

4. EMPTY CHAIR: Pull up an empty chair during the **Caring Time** at the close and ask God to fill this chair each week. Remember, by breaking into groups of four for the Bible Study time, you can grow numerically without feeling "too big" as a group.

The Group Leader needs an apprentice-in-training at all times so that the Apprentice can start a new "cell" when the group size is 12 or more.

SESSION 1
Orientation

PURPOSE: To get acquainted, to share your expectations, and decide on the ground rules for your group.

AGENDA: Gathering   Bible Study   Caring Time

OPEN

 GATHERING/10 Minutes/All Together

Leader: The purpose of the Gathering Time is to break the ice. Read the instructions for Step One and go first. Then read the Introduction (Step Two) and the instructions for the Bible Study.

Step One: SHOW AND TELL. Introduce yourself to the group by showing everyone a picture of your family. If you don't have any snapshots in your wallet/purse, tell them about your family: (1) ages, (2) interests, and (3) personalities.

INTRODUCTION

Step Two: WELCOME. Welcome to the wonderful world of parenting. In this course, you will discuss what parenting means at each stage of the process: birth, young childhood, older childhood, and teen years. You will also examine the issues of parental pain, parental expectations, and what it means to be part of the larger family of God. Taken together, these sessions will help us to share the pleasures and to take on the challenges of parenting. While parenthood is full of pleasures, it is also full of challenges which are sometimes intimidating, and which come at every stage of life.

Bill Cosby (in his book *Fatherhood*) says, "having a child is surely the most beautiful irrational act which two people in love can commit." While he writes this tongue-in-cheek, it is true that parenthood is one of the great challenges we face in this world. Certainly there are many joys of being parents, but many of us struggle with the challenges.

We may think of Steve Martin in the movie *Parenthood*, where he forces his son to play baseball and the son does poorly. The boy is embarrassed and mad at his father for making him play. Then Steve Martin's character envisions his son growing up to become a mass murderer, and blaming it on his father for making him play baseball when he didn't want to! This situation is taken to extreme for humor's sake, but we do wonder—what mistakes are we making that are scarring our children, maybe forever? Or we may think of Harry Chapin's song, "Cat's in the Cradle," where the father never has time for his son. He is always going to take his son "soon," but "soon" never comes. When the boy grows up, he doesn't have time for his aging father! We wonder every time we say "we don't have time" to our children, if this could end up being us.

Three parts to a session

Every session has three parts: (1) **Gathering**—to break the ice and introduce the topic, (2) **Bible Study**—to share your own study through a passage of Scripture, and (3) **Caring**—to decide what action you need to take in this area of your life and to support one another in this action.

In this course, the Bible Study approach is a little unique with a different focus. Usually, the focus of the Bible Study is the content of the passage. In this course, the focus will be on telling your "story," using the passage as a springboard.

📖 BIBLE STUDY/30 Minutes/Groups of 4

Leader: If you have more than seven in this session, we recommend groups of four—four to sit around the dining table, four around the kitchen table, and four around a folding table. Ask one person in each foursome to be the Convener and complete the Bible Study in the time allowed. Then regather for the Caring Time, allowing 20 minutes.

STUDY

In each foursome ask someone to be the Convener. Read the following Scripture, which is from Matthew 1:18–25. It is Matthew's account of the birth of Jesus. Go around on the first question. Then go around with the next question, working through the questionnaire. After 30 minutes, the Leader will call time and ask you to regather for the Caring Time.

[18] This is how the birth of Jesus Christ came about: His mother Mary was pledged to be married to Joseph, but before they came together, she was found to be with child through the Holy Spirit. [19] Because Joseph her husband was a righteous man and did not want to expose her to public disgrace, he had in mind to divorce her quietly.

[20] But after he had considered this, an angel of the Lord appeared to him in a dream and said, "Joseph son of David, do not be afraid to take Mary home as your wife, because what is conceived in her is from the Holy Spirit. [21] She will give birth to a son, and you are to give him the name Jesus, because he will save his people from their sins."

[22] All this took place to fulfill what the Lord had said through the prophet: [23] "The virgin will be with child and will give birth to a son, and they will call him Immanuel"—which means, "God with us."

[24] When Joseph woke up, he did what the angel of the Lord had commanded him and took Mary home as his wife. [25] But he had no union with her until she gave birth to a son. And he gave him the name Jesus.

Matthew 1:18–25, NIV

1. What do you think Joseph thought when he woke up from his dream?
- ❏ I'd better lay off the midnight snacks.
- ❏ I've been watching too much TV lately.
- ❏ I need to buy a new mattress.
- ❏ Mary must have some powerful connections.
- ❏ other: _____

2. What might have been Mary's thoughts during her pregnancy?
    - ❏ No one will believe me, especially Joseph.
    - ❏ What will the neighbors say?
    - ❏ My friends and family will abandon me.
    - ❏ Surely God must know what he's doing.
    - ❏ other: _____

3. What would you have done if you were Mary/Joseph?
    - ❏ left town fast
    - ❏ found the best psychiatrist in Bethlehem
    - ❏ trusted God for the next step
    - ❏ supported my spouse
    - ❏ other: _____

4. What was your reaction when you found out you were going to have your first baby?
    - ❏ It's about time.
    - ❏ You're kidding.
    - ❏ Can we afford this?
    - ❏ Oh no! Not yet!
    - ❏ other: _____

"If things go well with the family, life is worth living; when the family falters, life falls apart."
—Michael Novak

5. Reflecting back, how prepared were you to be a parent when you started out?
    - ❏ I was fully prepared.
    - ❏ I was basically prepared.
    - ❏ I knew a little bit.
    - ❏ I was totally unprepared.

6. How did you decide on a name for your firstborn child?

7. When Jesus was conceived, he came with a God-given set of expectations—that he would save his people from their sins. What phrase best describes the expectations you had for your first child when you learned that he or she was on the way?
    - ❏ Let's plan the Presidential campaign.
    - ❏ Is it too early to buy a baseball glove?
    - ❏ Does anybody know any good modeling agents?
    - ❏ Someone better warn Yale and Harvard, so they can start a recruiting war.
    - ❏ I just hope my child can survive my parenting.
    - ❏ other: _____

COMMENT

A recent Harris poll of 3,000 families found that:
- Parents' greatest concerns are drugs, alcohol, sexual promiscuity, and pregnancy.
- 86% of all parents expect their children will go to college.
- About 20% of families express dissatisfaction with family life, primarily due to financial burdens.

Other information:
- Studies show that first-time parents often romanticize parenthood.
- Fewer than 10% of American families have both a male breadwinner and a mother at home tending full-time to the family.
- Three-fifths of the mothers with children under the age of five have jobs outside the house.

♡ CARING TIME/20 Minutes/All Together

Leader: In this first session, take some time to discuss your expectations and to decide on the ground rules for your group. Then spend the remaining time in caring support for each other through sharing and prayer.

1. What motivated you to come to this group?
   ❒ curiosity
   ❒ a friend asked me
   ❒ I had nothing better to do.
   ❒ a nagging suspicion that I'd better get my life together

EXPECTATIONS

2. As you begin this group, what are some goals or expectations you have for this course? Choose two or three of the following expectations and add one of your own:

   ❒ to get to know some people who are willing to be open and honest about their struggles with parenting
   ❒ to relax and have fun—and forget parenting for awhile
   ❒ to see what the Bible has to say about parenting, and the strategies for family caring
   ❒ to deal with some of the difficulties I have in being a parent
   ❒ to deal with some of the fears I have in being a parent
   ❒ to see if God is saying anything to me about my life and his will for my life
   ❒ to learn some helpful hints in parenting from other parents
   ❒ to learn God's expectations for a healthy family
   ❒ to develop skills for strengthening family relationships
   ❒ other: _____

GROUND RULES

3. If you are going to commit the next six weeks or sessions to this group, what are some things you want understood by the group before you commit? Check two or three and add any of your own:

   ☐ **Attendance**: To take the group seriously, and to give the meetings priority.
   ☐ **Confidentiality**: Anything that is said in the meetings will not be repeated outside the group.
   ☐ **Accountability**: The group has the right to hold any member accountable for goals that member sets for himself/herself.
   ☐ **Responsibility**: Every group member accepts responsibility for the care and encouragement of the other group members.
   ☐ **Openness**: The group is open to any person that is willing to accept the ground rules.
   ☐ **Duration**: The group will commit to six more sessions. After this, the group will evaluate and recommit to another period if they wish to do so.

SHARING

Take a few minutes to share prayer requests with other group members. Go around and answer this question first:

"How can we help you in prayer this week?"

PRAYER

Take a moment to pray together. If you have not prayed aloud before, finish the sentence:

"Hello, God, this is... (first name). I want to thank you for..."

ACTION

1. Decide on where you are going to meet.

2. Ask someone to bring refreshments next week.

3. Encourage the group to invite a friend to the group next week—to fill the "empty chair" (see page 5).

SESSION 2
It's a Boy!

PURPOSE: To tell the story of the first time you became a parent.

AGENDA: Gathering   Bible Study   Caring Time

OPEN

GATHERING/10 Minutes/All Together

Leader: The purpose of the Gathering Time in this session is to help people get to know each other a bit better and to share something personal about themselves. We encourage you to be the first one to share with the group. Read the instructions for Step One and make sure everyone has a turn. Then read Step Two and move on to the Bible Study.

Step One: UNDER THE BIG TOP. Here is an ice-breaker from Serendipity's *Ice-Breakers and Heart-Warmers*. Look at the picture of the circus. If you imagine your family as a circus (that shouldn't be too hard to do!), which performers represent members of your family? If your small group was a circus, which performer would you be? Share your answers with the group.

INTRODUCTION

Step Two: IT'S A BOY! In our opening session, we talked about how each stage of parenting is full of pleasures as well as intimidating challenges. That is certainly true with the birth process itself. There is no other experience quite like the experience of giving birth. For most mothers (no matter how difficult their labor or how long their delivery), it is all soon forgotten when they see their newborn child. Fathers also experience great joy when they see the one they helped to create for the first time. With the opportunity that most fathers have today of being present in the delivery room, they are able to see their child the moment he or she emerges into the world.

With the pleasures come the challenges. The challenges of the birth stage mainly concern adjustment. Parents have to adjust to new financial stresses (Can we afford this child?) and to the new family dynamic (It's no longer just the two of us!). In this session, you will have the chance to share both the pleasures and the challenges of when you first became a parent.

LEADER: Choose the Option One Bible Study (below) or the Option Two Study (page 15).

There are two options for the Bible Study. Option One—for beginner groups—starts out with a familiar passage from Luke's Gospel on the birth of Jesus. We will discover some of the challenges Jesus' parents faced at that time. Option Two—for deeper groups—is a teaching passage from Paul's letter to the Romans. In that study, we will see the relationship between pleasures and challenges, both in our childbirth as well as in what God is "bringing to birth" in our world. Both tracks use a questionnaire approach to sharing that permits you to choose between multiple-choice options—with no right or wrong answers.

OPTION 1

 BIBLE STUDY/30 Minutes/Groups of 4

Leader: Help the group make a decision for Option One or Option Two. If there are more than seven in the group, subdivide into four's and rearrange your chairs so that everyone can participate. Ask one person in each foursome to be the Convener and complete the Bible Study in the time allowed. Then regather for the Caring Time, allowing 20 minutes.

Gospel Study/Humble Beginnings
Luke 2:1–7

STUDY

Read Luke 2:1–7 and discuss your responses to the following questions with your group. This version of Christ's birth, from Luke's Gospel, shows Luke's characteristic interest in historical detail.

2 *In those days Caesar Augustus issued a decree that a census should be taken of the entire Roman world.* ² *(This was the first census that took place while Quirinius was governor of Syria.)* ³ *And everyone went to his own town to register.*

⁴ *So Joseph also went up from the town of Nazareth in Galilee to Judea, to Bethlehem the town of David, because he belonged to the house and line of David.* ⁵ *He went there to register with Mary, who was pledged to be married to him and was expecting a child.* ⁶ *While they were there, the time came for the baby to be born,* ⁷ *and she gave birth to her firstborn, a son. She wrapped him in cloths and placed him in a manger, because there was no room for them in the inn.*

Luke 2:1–7, NIV

1. If you had been a reporter for *The Bethlehem Herald* at this time, interviewing the parents about this unusual birth, what would have been the first question you asked?
   - ❏ How did Mary ever hold up during that long trip?
   - ❏ Why didn't you call ahead for reservations?
   - ❏ How do you feel about the innkeeper putting you out here?
   - ❏ What are your hopes and fears for the future?

2. Pregnant. Broke. Homeless. What chance would you give Joseph and Mary of being good parents?
   - ❏ none
   - ❏ 50/50
   - ❏ uphill all the way
   - ❏ the best way to begin

3. Women: If you had been in Mary's situation, what would you have done?
   - ❏ withdrawn
   - ❏ returned to my family
   - ❏ cried a lot
   - ❏ relied on my inner resources
   - ❏ taken it out on my fiancé
   - ❏ other: _____

4. Men: If you had been in Joseph's situation, what would you have done?
   - ❏ walked out
   - ❏ stood by her
   - ❏ rose to the occasion
   - ❏ become depressed
   - ❏ asked for help
   - ❏ other: _____

"The first handshake in life is the greatest of all: the clasp of an infant around the finger of a parent."
—Mark Twain

5. How would their "humble" beginnings prepare them for parenting?
   - ❏ It gave them a dose of the real world.
   - ❏ It caused them to grow up fast.
   - ❏ It caused them to depend upon God.
   - ❏ It taught them that struggle is the best teacher.

6. How would you compare your start as a family to Mary and Joseph's?
   - ❏ We were not pregnant already.
   - ❏ We had it a bit easier.
   - ❏ At least we had a place to stay.
   - ❏ Our stories are similar.
   - ❏ I never thought about it.

7. If you could go back to the early days in your family life, would you?
   - ❏ It was sure easier then than it is now.
   - ❏ I'm glad we started out that way, but I would not go back.
   - ❏ in some ways "yes," and in other ways "no"
   - ❏ No way!
   - ❏ other: _____

8. What did you learn from the early days in your family life that you would like to pass on to your children?
   - ❏ keep a sense of humor
   - ❏ Struggles will deepen your relationship.
   - ❏ God didn't promise an easy path, but he promised his presence.
   - ❏ I would never give my kids advice.
   - ❏ other: _____

LEADER: When you have completed the Bible Study, move on to the Caring Time (page 18).

OPTION 2

Epistle Study/The Pain and the Hope
Romans 8:18–25

STUDY

Read Romans 8:18–25 and discuss the questions which follow with your group. In this passage, Paul compares the sufferings of the present time with the pain of childbirth, because it is pain that is full of hope for what is to come.

18 I consider that our present sufferings are not worth comparing with the glory that will be revealed in us. 19 The creation waits in eager expectation for the sons of God to be revealed. ²⁰ For the creation was subjected to frustration, not by its own choice, but by the will of the one who subjected it, in hope ²¹ that the creation itself will be liberated from its bondage to decay and brought into the glorious freedom of the children of God.

²² We know that the whole creation has been groaning as in the pains of childbirth right up to the present time. ²³ Not only so, but we ourselves, who have the firstfruits of the Spirit, groan inwardly as we wait eagerly for our adoption as sons, the redemption of our bodies. ²⁴ For in this hope we were saved. But hope that is seen is no hope at all. Who hopes for what he already has? ²⁵ But if we hope for what we do not yet have, we wait for it patiently.

Romans 8:18–25, NIV

1. What are your "present sufferings" as a parent?
    - ❐ washing smelly socks
    - ❐ cleaning messy lunch pails
    - ❐ chauffeuring children every day
    - ❐ dealing with runny noses and bloody knees
    - ❐ not being able to use my own telephone
    - ❐ other: _____

2. What comfort do you draw from this passage for your situation as a parent?
    - ❐ Life in this world is a pain.
    - ❐ All pain is like labor pain—it has a good purpose.
    - ❐ This imperfect world is "pregnant" with the new world God is creating.
    - ❐ If we put up with the pain now, it will be worth it later on.

3. When you were approaching the birth of your first child, what were the relative roles of hope and pain in the way you looked at your situation?
    - ❐ I was preoccupied with the pain—the discomforts of pregnancy and the knowledge of the labor pain to come!
    - ❐ I was preoccupied with the pain—putting up with the irritability of a pregnant wife!
    - ❐ I was focused fully on the hope of the child who was coming.
    - ❐ I vacillated back and forth between the hope and the pain.

4. As you think of the world which your child will inherit, what do you hope for, but do not yet see (see vv. 24–25)? Complete the following sentence, choosing the one most important to you. A world:
   - ❏ free of pollution and poison
   - ❏ with less violence and crime
   - ❏ where family values are emphasized
   - ❏ where education of children is valued more than the tools of war
   - ❏ other: _____

5. How do the assurances of this passage (see especially verses 18 and 21) affect your feelings about the future of your children?
   - ❏ Nice thoughts—but I'm still anxious and skeptical.
   - ❏ It helps, but I'd still like to see more of what I'm hoping for.
   - ❏ It gives me the peace I need to raise my children in this world.
   - ❏ other: _____

6. In the birth of your first child, what were the most difficult "pains" you had to suffer?
   - ❏ giving up our freedom to go where we wanted when we wanted
   - ❏ the financial drain
   - ❏ the physical pain
   - ❏ giving up the exclusive attention of my spouse
   - ❏ the changes in our sexual life
   - ❏ the anxiety of raising a child in this world
   - ❏ the fear of a child with physical or mental abnormalities

7. How strong were these pains you suffered (from question #6)?
   - ❏ Like the initial stages of labor—I barely knew they were there.
   - ❏ Like when the water breaks—they were hard but bearable.
   - ❏ Like hard, transitional labor—I wanted to say, "I've changed my mind!"
   - ❏ I don't even want to think about it!

LEADER: When you have completed the Bible Study, move on to the Caring Time (page 18).

8. If you could see one thing about your child's future that would assure you that it is all worth it, what would you like to see?

COMMENT

Christians in the early church had to deal with the reality of suffering. They were persecuted socially by the traditional religious leadership of the Jews, and later physically by the Roman government. In this passage, Paul tells the Christians of the Church at Rome that the sufferings we go through in this life are nothing compared to the joys that are in store for us.

He also assures them that the sufferings of this world are like labor pains that creation is going through on its way to the birth of a new world. It is a new world which God has in store. We live in hope that this will happen, even though we may not see hard evidence of it right now.

And so it is with parenting. We endure the pains, celebrate the joyous times, and always anticipate the future with hope.

♡ CARING TIME/20 Minutes/All Together

Leader: The purpose of the Caring Time in this session is to spend time in caring support for each other through Sharing and Prayer.

SHARING

1. Which type of music would best describe how your family got along this past week?
   - ❏ easy listening—everything went smoothly
   - ❏ classical—no surprises; the familiar routines
   - ❏ soft rock—a few bumps in the road
   - ❏ country—familiar, with a few nice surprises
   - ❏ jazz—I never knew what was coming next
   - ❏ rap—it was nonstop talking
   - ❏ heavy metal—it was really chaotic
   - ❏ other: _____

2. Take some time to share any personal prayer requests by answering the question:

   "Where do you need to grow in your life as a parent this week?"

PRAYER

Close with a short time of prayer, focusing on what people shared above. Go around in a circle and give everyone an opportunity to pray. If you want to pray in silence when it is your turn, say the word "Amen" when you have finished your prayer, so that the next person will know when to start.

ACTION

On an index card, write your first name and one prayer request you have for your family. Randomly distribute the cards, and ask everyone to pray for the person on their card throughout the coming week.

SESSION 3
Diaper Days

PURPOSE: To discover that rearing children is both a pleasurable and a painful venture.

AGENDA: Gathering   Bible Study   Caring Time

OPEN

GATHERING/10 Minutes/All Together

Leader: Read the instructions for Step One and make sure everyone has a chance to respond. As people get to know one another, they will feel secure and free to share something personal. We encourage you to set the stage and share first. Then read the Introduction in Step Two and move on to the Bible Study.

Step One: I'M JUST A KID! You're 11 years old. Who are you? What do you like to do? If the group could meet you as an 11-year-old kid, what would you be like? Look at the following situations and tell the group your response to one of them:

- ❏ It's your 11th birthday! Yum, a birthday cake! What kind is it? You blow out the candles easily. What did you wish for? What is your "dream" present?
- ❏ Your father (or guardian) is returning from a day of work. What does he do? What do you want to be when you grow up?
- ❏ Yahoo! The teachers are at a convention today! What are you going to do? Who do you want to do it with?
- ❏ It's Friday. Your best friend is coming over to spend the night. What is his/her name? What is he/she like? What do you like most about this friend?
- ❏ Summer is here! Where is your family going on vacation? What's your favorite thing about this place? Are you going there by car? What's it like in the car?
- ❏ The recess bell has rung! What are you going to do?
- ❏ Think of a kindly older person on your street. How would they describe you when you were eleven?

INTRODUCTION

Step Two: DIAPER DAYS. Once a child is born, we as parents have both new pleasures and new challenges. The new pleasures center around seeing our child develop his or her own unique personality. We take delight in a special smile we come to understand. We experience what our child adds to our life.

The new challenges, on the other hand, center around discipline. What can we do to make sure our child grows into a loving, well-adjusted adult who knows how to take a responsible role in our world? One of the first things we need to do in order to meet this challenge is to enable our child to trust us. Child psychologist Erik Erikson tells us that one of the key issues in a child's first year of life is developing trust. Can our child trust us to provide what he or she needs, both physically and emotionally? Can our child trust us to discipline out of love rather than striking out in anger? These are indeed challenges for us as we seek to be good parents.

LEADER: Choose the Option One Bible Study (below) or the Option Two Study (page 24).

This session will help us to talk about early childhood and its associated challenges. In the Option One Study (from Luke's Gospel), we will examine the presentation of Mary and Joseph's newborn in the Temple. We will also examine what similar acts we can do for our children to "present them to the Lord." In the Option Two Study, we will learn about Paul's parental model in his letter to the Thessalonians. Both studies will provide an opportunity to discuss your early parenting days.

Remember, the purpose of the Bible Study is to share your own story. Use this opportunity to deal with some issues in your life.

OPTION 1

 # BIBLE STUDY/30 Minutes/Groups of 4

Leader: Help the group choose Option One or Option Two for their Bible Study. If there are seven or more in the group, encourage them to move into groups of four. Ask one person in each group to be the Convener. The Convener guides the sharing and makes sure that each group member has an opportunity to answer every question.

Gospel Study/Presented at the Temple
Luke 2:21–40

STUDY

Read Luke 2:21–40 and discuss your responses to the following questions with your group. This story (found only in Luke's Gospel) concerns Jesus' parents as they fulfill one of the religious obligations of new parents.

²¹ On the eighth day, when it was time to circumcise him, he was named Jesus, the name the angel had given him before he had been conceived.

²² When the time of their purification according to the Law of Moses had been completed, Joseph and Mary took him to Jerusalem to present him to the Lord ²³ (as it is written in the Law of the Lord, "Every firstborn male is to be consecrated to the Lord"), ²⁴ and to offer a sacrifice in keeping with what is said in the Law of the Lord: "a pair of doves or two young pigeons."

²⁵ Now there was a man in Jerusalem called Simeon, who was righteous and devout. He was waiting for the consolation of Israel, and the Holy Spirit was upon him. ²⁶ It had been revealed to him by the Holy Spirit that he would not die before he had seen the Lord's Christ. ²⁷ Moved by the Spirit, he went into the temple courts. When the parents brought in the child Jesus to do for him what the custom of the Law required, ²⁸ Simeon took him in his arms and praised God, saying:

> ²⁹ "Sovereign Lord, as you have promised,
>   you now dismiss your servant in peace.
> ³⁰ For my eyes have seen your salvation,
> ³¹   which you have prepared in the sight of all people,
> ³² a light for revelation to the Gentiles
>   and for glory to your people Israel."

³³ The child's father and mother marveled at what was said about him. ³⁴ Then Simeon blessed them and said to Mary, his mother: "This child is destined to cause the falling and rising of many in Israel, and to be a sign that will be spoken against, ³⁵ so that the thoughts of many hearts will be revealed. And a sword will pierce your own soul too."

³⁶ There was also a prophetess, Anna, the daughter of Phanuel, of the tribe of Asher. She was very old; she had lived with her husband seven years after her marriage, ³⁷ and then was a widow until she was eighty-four. She never left the temple but worshiped night and day, fasting and praying. ³⁸ Coming up to them at that very moment, she gave thanks to God and spoke about the child to all who were looking forward to the redemption of Jerusalem.

³⁹ When Joseph and Mary had done everything required by the Law of the Lord, they returned to Galilee to their own town of Nazareth. ⁴⁰ And the child grew and became strong; he was filled with wisdom, and the grace of God was upon him.

Luke 2:21–40, NIV

1. If you had been Joseph or Mary and experienced the events in this passage, what would have been the first thing you wrote down in your diary when you returned?
   - ❏ "Everybody loved him—I was so proud!"
   - ❏ "Old people say such strange things sometimes!"
   - ❏ "I never had so much to thank the Lord for as this time!"
   - ❏ "I wonder what that man meant about a sword piercing my soul?"

2. Why were Mary and Joseph so careful to do "everything required by the Law of the Lord"?
   - ❏ They really needed to get out of the house, and this was a good opportunity.
   - ❏ They wanted to look good.
   - ❏ They didn't want to be punished.
   - ❏ They were good Jews—it was their tradition.
   - ❏ They wanted to be extra-careful to raise their child right.
   - ❏ other: _____

3. What was the first "out-of-the-house" trip you took with your newborn?

4. When you took your first newborn out of the house, what reactions did you get from the people you met?
   - ❏ Gee, he/she looks like mom.
   - ❏ Gee, he/she looks like dad.
   - ❏ lots of silly baby talk
   - ❏ lots of child-rearing advice
   - ❏ other parents compared notes with us
   - ❏ the classic question—"Is he/she a *good* baby?"

5. Why do you suppose this was such a meaningful occasion for Simeon?
   - ❏ He had waited so long for this moment.
   - ❏ He expected to see the Christ—God's anointed one.
   - ❏ God had not forgotten his promise.
   - ❏ He marvelled at how God could use a baby to bring his salvation.

6. What would be the crowning joy for you in old age?
   - ❏ to see my children's children
   - ❏ to strike it rich
   - ❏ to look back on a life full of surprises
   - ❏ to leave the world a better place in which to live
   - ❏ to feel I have done God's will

"[Good parents are] not afraid to be momentarily disliked by children during the act of enforcing rules."
—Jean Laird

7. Which of the following acts were (are) on your list for "doing everything required" by the Lord?
   - ❏ circumcision
   - ❏ taking my child to church
   - ❏ baptism, christening, or dedication
   - ❏ loving my child
   - ❏ spending lots of time with my child
   - ❏ praying for my child
   - ❏ building a trusting relationship with my child
   - ❏ disciplining my child
   - ❏ teaching my child about God
   - ❏ providing for my child's education
   - ❏ providing for my child's physical needs

8. Which of the acts in the list above were (are) your top two priorities?

9. Which of the actions on your list did (do) you have the hardest time doing?

LEADER: When you have completed the Bible Study, move on to the Caring Time (page 26).

10. Do you think God has a plan and purpose for your life as a parent like he did for Mary and Joseph?
    - ❏ not at all
    - ❏ probably—wish I knew what it was
    - ❏ in a way
    - ❏ definitely, and I'm still discovering it
    - ❏ maybe, but not the same plan

COMMENT

Every culture and society has its rituals surrounding a birth. In our culture, we have baby showers before the birth and visits to the hospital after it. The most important tradition for many of us is the day our baby is taken to church for the christening, baptism, or dedication.

There are two Old Testament rituals in this passage. First is the ritual of presenting oneself for purification following childbirth. For 40 days after giving birth to her son, Mary was forbidden to go to the Temple or to participate in any religious service. Afterwards, she offered a sacrifice of two birds for her cleansing.

Second is the ritual of the redemption of the firstborn (see Ex. 13:2). In commemoration of the events surrounding the Passover, the firstborn male in every Jewish family was to be set apart for God. Because Mary and Joseph brought Jesus to the Temple (as opposed to simply paying the priest), perhaps it was their intention to dedicate Jesus to God. This is similar to Samuel (1 Sam. 1:11, 22, 28), who was offered to the service of the priests at the Temple when he was older.

The responses of Simeon and Anna took Mary and Joseph by surprise. Simeon and Anna had waited on God with consistent prayer for him to bring about the promises of the Messianic age (Isa. 40:1–11; 49:8–13). With Jesus' presentation at the Temple, they knew that their prayers had been answered and that they could die in peace. But their prophetic words raised more questions in the hearts of Mary and Joseph as to who their son really was.

OPTION 2

Epistle Study/Parental Model
1 Thessalonians 2:6–12

STUDY

Read 1 Thessalonians 2:6–12 and discuss your responses to the following questions with your group. This passage is Paul's recounting of the way he dealt with the Thessalonians when he started the church in their city.

> *⁶ As apostles of Christ we could have been a burden to you, ⁷ but we were gentle among you, like a mother caring for her little children. ⁸ We loved you so much that we were delighted to share with you not only the gospel of God but our lives as well, because you had become so dear to us. ⁹ Surely you remember, brothers, our toil and hardship; we worked night and day in order not to be a burden to anyone while we preached the gospel of God to you.*
> *¹⁰ You are witnesses, and so is God, of how holy, righteous and blameless we were among you who believed. ¹¹ For you know that we dealt with each of you as a father deals with his own children, ¹² encouraging, comforting and urging you to live lives worthy of God, who calls you into his kingdom and glory.*
> *1 Thessalonians 2:6–12, NIV*

1. If you had been one of those who received this letter, what would your reaction have been?
   ☐ I already have a mother, thank you.
   ☐ what a guilt trip
   ☐ It's nice to have someone care so much.
   ☐ What is he up to?

> "The chances are that you will never be elected president of the country, write the Great American novel, make a million dollars, stop pollution, end racial conflict, or save the world. However valid it may be to work at any of these goals, there is one of higher priority—to be an effective parent."
> —Landrum R. Bolling

LEADER: When you have completed the Bible Study, move on to the Caring Time (page 26).

2. In speaking to the church in Thessalonica, why do you think Paul uses this parental imagery? He wants to reassure the church that:
   - ❑ They are people of God.
   - ❑ They wouldn't be a burden.
   - ❑ They were dealt with fairly and lovingly.
   - ❑ They were only being encouraged and comforted.

3. Which three of the following characteristics do you think are most important for parents to possess? Why?
   - ❑ flexibility
   - ❑ patience
   - ❑ gentleness
   - ❑ authority
   - ❑ kindness
   - ❑ faith
   - ❑ love
   - ❑ organization
   - ❑ firmness
   - ❑ perseverance
   - ❑ perfection
   - ❑ wisdom
   - ❑ unselfishness
   - ❑ sense of humor
   - ❑ sympathy
   - ❑ understanding

4. Which two of the characteristics above do (did) your parents possess?

   my mother: _____
   _____

   my father: _____
   _____

5. What is your fondest memory of how your mother or grandmother cared for you when you were a child?

6. What is your fondest memory of how your father or grandfather encouraged or comforted you when you were a child?

7. Who in your life urged you to live your life in God's ways?

8. Which of the parental functions that Paul talks about in this letter do you believe you do best as a parent?
   - ❑ showing gentleness
   - ❑ sharing my life
   - ❑ working night and day for my family
   - ❑ encouraging
   - ❑ comforting
   - ❑ urging my children to live lives worthy of God

9. Which of the functions above do you have the hardest time fulfilling?

COMMENT

Studies have shown that babies need human touch in order to survive (let alone thrive) in life. Paul's letter to the church in Thessalonica states that the same is true for infants in the faith.

Like a mother, Paul states that he gently loves those in the faith. In doing so, he will withhold no care from them. Like a father, Paul will encourage, comfort, and urge them in the faith. Undoubtedly, Paul's use of parental imagery (in caring for those in the church) is based on the ways God cares for us. Most importantly, they provide a wonderful model for parents as well.

CARING TIME/20 Minutes/All Together

Leader: Bring all of the foursomes back together for a time of caring. Follow the three steps below.

SHARING

Take some time to share any personal prayer requests by answering the question:

"If you knew you could not fail, what would you like to change in your relationship with your parents?"

PRAYER

Close with a short time of prayer, remembering the requests that have been shared. If you would like to pray in silence, say the word "Amen" when you have finished your prayer, so that the next person will know when to start.

ACTION

Turn to the person next to you and tell them one thing you want to change this week about your parenting (or home situation) to be a more loving parent. For example, "Pray that I have more patience with my children," or "Pray that I take more time to spend with my son," or "Pray that I will be more supportive of my spouse."

SESSION 4
He Got That from You

PURPOSE: To develop a practical framework for loving, effective parenting.

AGENDA: Gathering   Bible Study   Caring Time

OPEN

GATHERING/10 Minutes/All Together

Leader: Read the instructions for Step One. Continue to be sensitive to group members as they share, and set the pace by going first. Then read Step Two and move on to the Bible Study.

Step One: PEOPLE PIE. The people in our lives are one of our most precious resources. Of all the different relationships in your life, who gets the most of your time, love, energy, and money? Use the circles below to make pie charts which show who gets what from you:

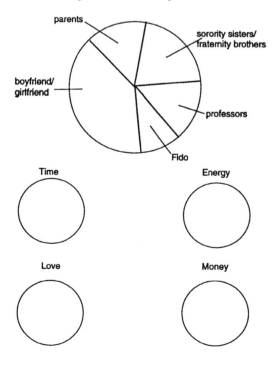

27

INTRODUCTION

Step Two: HE GOT THAT FROM YOU. Having a child is one thing; raising a child is quite another. Interestingly enough, very few parents have received any "formal" training in raising children. Most of us "wing it" and often make many of the same decisions our parents made. But raising children today is different than it was for our parents.

Today, many parents feel ambivalent about raising children. The demands of a job or career can place excessive stress and pressure on couples (and on single parents, who want to be conscientious in raising their children). In fact, recent studies have shown that most mothers work because they have to—they don't have a choice. About half of these working mothers feel cheated because they are missing out on the best years of their kids' lives. It is little wonder that many young couples have chosen to have fewer children.

But despite the numerous obstacles in parenting, many families today are thriving. In his book, *Secrets of Strong Families*, Nick Stinnett explains that there are six qualities which are consistently found in strong families.

- **Commitment:** "They have a sense of being a team."
- **Appreciation:** "These folks help each other feel good about themselves."
- **Communication:** "They spend a lot of time talking and listening."
- **Time Together:** "These families eat, work, play, and talk together."
- **Spiritual Health:** "It is a unifying force that enables them to reach out in love and compassion to others."
- **Coping Skills:** "Some of their coping skills are: seeing something positive in the crises, pulling together, being flexible, drawing on spiritual and communication strengths, and getting help from friends and professionals."

The later childhood period is a time of increasing independence. It starts in infancy. First the infant thinks he or she is one with the mother. Later (when the infant learns this is not true), he or she experiences "separation anxiety," when he or she is away from parents or caregivers. But as the child gets older, he or she learns that being a separate individual has its benefits as well as its anxieties. The child begins to enjoy and assert his or her independence, which sometimes results in increasing problems with disobedience. During this time, both parents sometimes wish they could avoid the primary responsibility for these errant ways. "He got that from you!", often said in jest (but sometimes quite seriously), becomes our escape clause.

However, this period is also an important time of development of the child's own conscience. That means that an important parental role during this time is helping the child to develop his or her own faith. Toward the end of this period, children begin to think abstractly, which helps them to understand the essential concept of salvation.

LEADER: Choose the Option One Bible Study (below) or the Option Two Study (page 32).

This session focuses on parenting during late childhood. Much of the practical framework for loving, effective parenting comes from the Bible. In Option One, we will look at a parenting crisis which Mary and Joseph had during Jesus' youth. In Option Two, we will look at some advice about discipline from Hebrews, and we will consider its relevance for parenting children who are developing their own conscience. Remember, the purpose of the Bible Study is to share your own story. Use this opportunity to deal with issues in your life in this support group.

OPTION 1

 BIBLE STUDY/30 Minutes/Groups of 4

Leader: Help the group decide on an Option One or Option Two Bible Study. If there are more than seven people, divide into groups of four, and ask one person in each group to be the Convener. Finish the Bible Study in 30 minutes, and gather the groups together for the Caring Time.

Gospel Study/Growing Pains
Luke 2:41–52

STUDY

Read Luke 2:41–52 and discuss your responses to the following questions with your group. This story is the only one in the Bible about Jesus between his infancy and adulthood.

[41] Every year his parents went to Jerusalem for the Feast of the Passover. [42] When he was twelve years old, they went up to the Feast, according to the custom. [43] After the Feast was over, while his parents were returning home, the boy Jesus stayed behind in Jerusalem, but they were unaware of it. [44] Thinking he was in their company, they traveled on for a day. Then they began looking for him among their relatives and friends. [45] When they did not find him, they went back to Jerusalem to look for him. [46] After three days they found him in the temple courts, sitting among the teachers, listening to them and asking them questions. [47] Everyone who heard him was amazed at his understanding and his answers. [48] When his parents saw him, they were astonished. His

mother said to him, "Son, why have you treated us like this? Your father and I have been anxiously searching for you."

⁴⁹ "Why were you searching for me?" he asked. "Didn't you know I had to be in my Father's house?" ⁵⁰ But they did not understand what he was saying to them.

⁵¹ Then he went down to Nazareth with them and was obedient to them. But his mother treasured all these things in her heart. ⁵² And Jesus grew in wisdom and stature, and in favor with God and men.

Luke 2:41–52, NIV

1. How would you describe Jesus' behavior?
   - ❏ He disobeyed his parents.
   - ❏ He put his heavenly Father's concerns over his earthly parents' concerns.
   - ❏ He was oblivious to his parents.
   - ❏ He behaved like a typical 12-year-old.

2. What do you think of Mary and Joseph's behavior in these verses?
   - ❏ They were negligent parents.
   - ❏ They didn't know their son very well.
   - ❏ They were confused by who Jesus really was.
   - ❏ They were "laid-back" parents.
   - ❏ They behaved like any good parents would.

3. How do you think Mary and Joseph felt as they searched for Jesus?
   - ❏ They were certain everything would be OK.
   - ❏ They were probably "worried sick."
   - ❏ They were feeling guilty about leaving Jesus.
   - ❏ They were probably quite angry.
   - ❏ They were trusting God to work it all out.

4. If you had been Mary or Joseph, what would you have said to Jesus when you found him?
   - ❏ "Don't you ever do that again!"
   - ❏ "How could you have just run off like that?"
   - ❏ "You had us worried sick!"
   - ❏ "You're grounded for a month!"
   - ❏ "I understand why you're here in the Temple."

> *"Back when we started out, we had three hard and fast child-rearing principles, but no children. Now, we have three children, but no principles."*
> —Anonymous

5. How was this incident important to Jesus' development as a preteen?
   - ❏ It showed he could take care of himself.
   - ❏ It showed he was developing his own faith.
   - ❏ It showed he was thinking for himself.
   - ❏ He had finished school and could now teach his elders.
   - ❏ It showed he knew who he was—the unique Son of God.
   - ❏ other: _____

6. What was your first significant time apart from your parents, or a "coming of age" experience as a teenager? What was significant about it?
   - ❏ summer camp in the mountains
   - ❏ confirmation class (or a spiritual retreat)
   - ❏ field trip to "the big city"
   - ❏ getting a summer job with room and board away from home
   - ❏ other: _____

7. At age 12, what was the most difficult parenting problem you posed for your parents?
   - ❏ The outbreak of puberty posed innumerable problems.
   - ❏ I raised religious questions my parents couldn't answer.
   - ❏ My peers began to influence me in ways my parents didn't like.
   - ❏ I discovered the opposite sex, and that raised new relational problems.
   - ❏ I began to rebel more often, raising new discipline problems.

8. If your children have reached their late childhood years, what do you think you'll really treasure from these years?

9. What are your biggest anxieties about parenting children of this age group?
   - ❏ the increasing influence of peers
   - ❏ they're almost teenagers
   - ❏ school performance
   - ❏ the availability of alcohol and drugs
   - ❏ sexual promiscuity
   - ❏ violence in the schools
   - ❏ the prevalence of child abuse
   - ❏ whether they will still want to be around the family
   - ❏ other: _____

LEADER: When you have completed the Bible Study, move on to the Caring Time (page 35).

10. What comfort can you find concerning these anxieties in our biblical story?
- ❏ Even Jesus' parents had to go through this.
- ❏ Developing independence is necessary in growing up.
- ❏ It reminds me of how children sometimes mature without us noticing it.
- ❏ other: _____

COMMENT

You might call this a biblical version of *Home Alone*—Mary and Joseph both assumed that Jesus was with the other, only to find him missing. When they retraced their steps, they found him in a surprising situation. Their little boy was asking some rather penetrating questions of the teachers.

One can only imagine Mary and Joseph looking at each other and thinking about Jesus' typical boyhood, then saying to each other, "Who is that boy? And what has he done with our son?" Despite the special circumstances surrounding Jesus' birth, Mary and Joseph were only beginning to discover the uniqueness of their son.

OPTION 2

Epistle Study/Discipline
Hebrews 12:5–11

STUDY

Read Hebrews 12:5–11 and discuss your responses to the following questions with your group. This passage was written to Christians who were about to be persecuted, in order to help them to see hard times as events which God uses to discipline us.

⁵ And you have forgotten that word of encouragement that addresses you as sons:

> *"My son, do not make light of the Lord's discipline,*
> *and do not lose heart when he rebukes you,*
> *⁶ because the Lord disciplines those he loves,*
> *and he punishes everyone he accepts as a son."*

⁷ Endure hardship as discipline; God is treating you as sons. For what son is not disciplined by his father? ⁸ If you are not disciplined (and everyone undergoes discipline), then you are illegitimate children and not true sons. ⁹ Moreover, we have all had human fathers who disciplined us and we respected them for it. How much more should we submit to the

20 courses/7 to 13 weeks
WHERE YOU HURT AND STRUGGLE

These "personal need" courses are designed for non-threatening mutual help groups with life-experience leaders. Each session has two tracks: TRACK 1—for beginner groups with easy-sharing questionnaires, and TRACK 2—with deeper Bible study. A leader TRAINING MANUAL is available.

DESIGNED FOR:
- On-going groups
- Retreats
- Special needs groups
- Elective Sunday school classes

MARRIAGE ENRICHMENT COURSES
- Engaged: Are You Fit to be Tied?
- Infertility: Coping With the Pain of Childlessness
- Newly Married: How to Have a Great First Year

RECOVERY COURSES
- Addictive Lifestyles: Breaking Free
- Co-Dependency: Breaking Free From Entangled Relationships
- 12-Steps: The Path to Wholeness

PARENTING COURSES
- Blended Families: Yours, Mine, Ours
- Parenting Adolescents: Easing the Way to Adulthood
- Parents of Pre-Schoolers: From Car Seats to Kindergarten
- Learning Disabilities: Parenting the Misunderstood
- Single Parents: Flying Solo

SPECIAL NEEDS COURSES
- Compassion Fatigue: Worn Out From Caring
- Dealing With Grief & Loss: Hope in the Midst of Pain
- Divorce Recovery: Picking Up the Pieces
- Golden Years: Riding the Crest
- Midlife: The Crisis That Brings Renewal
- Single Again: Life After Divorce
- Stress Management: Finding the Balance
- Unemployed/Unfulfilled: Down, But Not Out
- Waist Watchers: Trimming Down to Size

LEADER TRAINING
- Support and Recovery Group Training Manual

What if we don't have any of these needs in our church?

Just offer these courses and see who signs up.

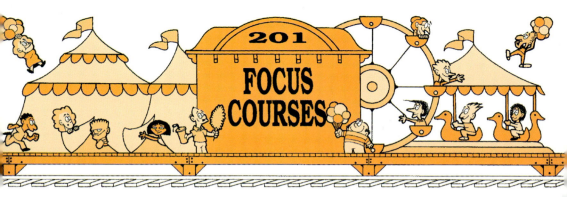

201 FOCUS COURSES

16 courses/7 to 13 weeks
AROUND LIFESTYLE

Pick the topic you are interested in. Reach out to others with this interest. It's called an affinity group—people with the same interest.

Each session (after the first one) has two levels or tracks: TRACK 1—for beginner groups with easy-sharing Bible questionnaires like 101 courses, and TRACK 2—with deeper Bible study. Or take both tracks and make it a 13-week course.

DESIGNED FOR:
- Beginner Groups (track 1)
- On-going Groups (track 2)
- Sunday school classes
- Elective courses
- Retreats

WHOL-I-NESS
Holy, Wholly, Holey, Dimensions of a Whole Person

PARENTING
Not Just a Stroll in the Park, Stages of Family Life

MAN TO MAN
Beyond Football and the Weather, Things Men Are Afraid to Talk About

SINGLES
The Secret Behind the Smile, Issues Vital to Singles

SELF-PORTRAIT
Recognizing Your Potential, Mirrors Into Knowing Yourself

STRESSED OUT
Hot, Dry and About to Crumble, Prescriptions for the Emotionally Drained

MARKETPLACE
Surviving in the Real World, Habits of a Highly Effective Christian

JESUS
Up Front and Personal, Studies on the Life of Christ

CORE VALUES
Changing From the Inside Out, Truths to Challenge Your Thinking

GIFTS & CALLING
Targeting Your Passion, Keys to a Highly Energized Life

WARFARE
Overcoming the Dragon, Studies on Spiritual Conflicts

BASICS
Confirming What I Believe, Essentials in the Christian Faith

RELATIONSHIPS
Becoming a Caring Community, Stages to Building Relationships

WOMAN TO WOMAN
Beyond the Stereotypes, Issues Women Need to Talk About

COUPLES
Making a Good Marriage Better, Skills for Effective Communications

TROUBLES
Keeping the Alligators at Bay, Strategies for Draining the Swamp

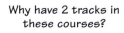 Why have 2 tracks in these courses?

 So you can switch back to Beginner Bible study when new people come.

CHECK YOUR BOOK STORE OR CALL 1-800-525-9563

6 courses/6 weeks
TO START GROUPS *Right!*

Becoming a group is easy and fun with these 6-session courses. Each session starts with an ice-breaker and ends with caring time. The Bible study is designed to help you share your own spiritual story through stories in the Bible. A two-part questionnaire guides the discussion with multiple-choice options to make sharing easy and fun. All you need to add is coffee!

DESIGNED FOR:
- **Beginner Groups**
- **Membership Classes**
- **Affinity Groups**
- **Retreats**

ALL ABOARD:
Six Sessions for Kicking-Off a Group
- First Call!
- Tell Us About Yourself
- Now That We're Together
- Thanks For Sharing
- How Are You Doing?
- Where Do We Go From Here?

WELCOME:
Six Sessions for Getting Involved in Your Church
- How Do You Do?
- Home Sweet Home
- What's Up
- Discovering Your Gifts
- Work in Progress
- Next!

BEGINNINGS:
Six Sessions for Spiritual Beginnings
- Getting Acquainted
- When Did Jesus Become More Than a Name?
- How's It Going in Your Life?
- How Can We Help You in Prayer?
- What is God Asking You to Do?
- Do We Want to Continue?

WOMEN:
Six Sessions for Starting a Women's Group
- Ready ... Set ... Go ...
- Stressed for Success
- Face Value
- U-Turn Permitted
- Maxed Out
- Now What?

MEN:
Six Sessions for Starting a Men's Group
- Male Bonding
- Initiation Rites
- Role Models
- Parental Expectations
- Testing
- Fourth and Goal

COUPLES:
Six Sessions to Begin a Couples' Group
- Our Wedding
- Our Courtship
- Our Honeymoon
- Our Humble Beginnings
- Our Love Life
- Our Tomorrow

Why take 6 weeks to say "hello"?

Because it takes time to become a group.

CHECK YOUR LOCAL BOOK STORE OR CALL 1-800-525-9563

1 course/6 weeks
TO END A GROUP Graciously!

Saying "goodbye" is just as important as saying "hello," and this course is designed to help your small group feel good about ending your group meetings.

In six countdown sessions, you will reminisce over the high points in your life together and celebrate what God has done. The Bible studies are designed to discover your gifts and what God is calling you to do next.

Then, you will plan your next step in your spiritual journey and the group will support you in starting out.

Graduation completes the lifecycle of a group. As a group you will encourage each other and help one another look at the future. Your group may decide to launch a ministry or tackle a mission's project—whatever you decide, your group is there to affirm its members.

DESIGNED FOR:
- Ending Groups
- Leadership Training
- Planning Retreats

But we don't want to quit!

You can always be a reunion group and celebrate 3 times a year.

CHECK YOUR BOOK STORE OR CALL 1-800-525-9563

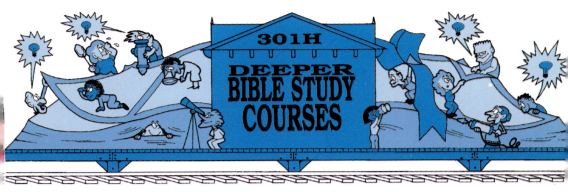

8 courses/1 or 2 semesters
TO COMBINE TEACHING AND GROUPS

This series is designed for churches that want to link their small groups to the teaching from the pastor, like the early church model of "temple courts ... and house to house." Each course comes with a PASTOR/TEACHER book and a STUDENT book. In the Student book, there are worksheets to complete at home and a Group Agenda for the small group meeting. Each course is designed for 1 semester, except for Corinthians and Romans which have 2 semesters.

DESIGNED FOR:
- Church-wide groups
- Elective Sunday school classes
- Deeper Bible study groups with homework

ONE-SEMESTER COURSES
- Ephesians (7 or 13 wks)
- Philippians (7 or 13 wks)
- James (7 or 13 wks)
- 1 John (includes 2 & 3 John, 7 or 13 wks)
- 1 Peter (1 to 10 wks)
- 1 & 2 Timothy (7 to 13 wks)

TWO-SEMESTER COURSES
- Romans (13 to 28 weeks)
- 1 Corinthians (13 to 27 weeks)

Designed for a "Two-Semester" School Year

1ST SEMESTER
Sept. 15 — Dec. 15

2ND SEMESTER
Feb. 1 — May 1

Photos by Troy Rowe

CHECK YOUR BOOK STORE OR CALL 1-800-525-9563

12 courses/7 to 27 weeks
TO UNDERSTAND THE BIBLE

When your group wants to go deeper in Bible study but doesn't have time for homework, this is the series for you. Each session has a built-in lap-top format with everything you need for the Bible study in a double-page layout: the TEXT of the Bible, GROUP QUESTIONS on three levels of sharing, and REFERENCE NOTES if you run across a difficult word. Beginners and Bible experts can meet on a level playing field.

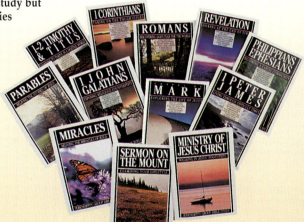

DESIGNED FOR:
- On-going Groups
- Bible study groups with NO homework
- Elective courses

SINGLE BOOKS OF THE BIBLE
(With 2 study plans to choose from)
- 1 Corinthians (13 or 24 weeks)
- Gospel of Mark (13 or 26 weeks)
- Romans (15 or 27 weeks)
- Revelation (13 or 26 weeks)
- Miracles (13 weeks)
- Parables (13 weeks)
- Sermon on the Mount (13 weeks)
- Ministry of Jesus Christ (13 weeks)

COMBINATION BOOKS
(With 4 study plans to choose from)
- 1 Peter (8 or 10 weeks) James (8 or 12 weeks)
- 1 John (5 or 8 weeks) & Galatians (7 or 13 weeks)
- Philippians (8 or 10 weeks) & Ephesians (8 or 11 weeks)
- 1 Timothy (6 or 9 weeks), 2 Timothy (6 weeks) & Titus (4 weeks)

What is the lap-top format? Sounds like a computer!

It's everything you need for group discussion in a double-page format.

8-HOUR or WEEKEND SMALL GROUP RETREAT KIT

A Serendipity Seminar is now available for you to hold your own training day for small group leaders.

The KIT includes:
- Director's book: a 48-page, fully illustrated procedure book with minute-by-minute instructions.
- Tablet with 50 handouts for each of 4 sessions.
- Two Advertising Posters
- Ten Advertising Buttons
- Ten Solid Brass Serendipity Crosses for the commissioning service at the close.

EXTRA MATERIALS ARE AVAILABLE

IN 8 HOURS YOU WILL LEARN:
- How to start a small group
- What to do in the first few weeks
- How to get acquainted
- How to study the Bible as a group
- How to move across the disclosure scale from easy sharing to heavy sharing
- How to pray for the empty chair and reach out to new people
- How to multiply when you are ready
- How to use the Serendipity small group materials

CHECK YOUR BOOK STORE OR CALL 1-800-525-9563

> **Serendipity is the facility of making happy chance discoveries.**
>
> —*Horace Walpole, 1743.*

Father of our spirits and live! ¹⁰ Our fathers disciplined us for a little while as they thought best; but God disciplines us for our good, that we may share in his holiness. ¹¹ No discipline seems pleasant at the time, but painful. Later on, however, it produces a harvest of righteousness and peace for those who have been trained by it.

Hebrews 12:5–11, NIV

1. If you had been one of the Christians who received this letter and heard it for the first time, what would have been your reaction to this passage?
   - ❏ It sounds like we are about to catch it good.
   - ❏ At least he didn't say, "This is going to hurt me more than it hurts you."
   - ❏ If this is what it means to be a "son," I'm not sure I want to be one.
   - ❏ This writer really knows what it's like to be a parent.
   - ❏ It's true of my experience of discipline—I've learned much from hardship.

2. Which of the arguments for the necessity of discipline do you find most convincing in this passage?
   - ❏ It's an indication of love.
   - ❏ We respect those who discipline us.
   - ❏ Discipline results in righteousness and peace.
   - ❏ other: _____

3. What discipline do you appreciate now that you sometimes resented as a child?
   - ❏ practicing a musical instrument
   - ❏ getting my school work in on time
   - ❏ paying the "consequences" for my mistakes
   - ❏ having a place for everything and everything in its place
   - ❏ not overspending my allowance

4. How has God disciplined you in the past? How did his discipline lead to peace for you?

5. How did you respond to God's discipline?
   - ❏ I became resentful and angry.
   - ❏ It made me feel hurt and unloved.
   - ❏ I felt special and loved.
   - ❏ It made me a more responsible Christian.
   - ❏ other: _____

*"The rules for parents are but three ...
Love,
Limit,
And let them be!"*
—Elaine M. Ward

6. Of all the ways your parents disciplined you, which method do you now think was the most effective? Why?

7. How would you describe your parenting methods?
   ❒ They're more strict than most parents I know.
   ❒ They're about the same as most parents I know.
   ❒ They're less strict than most parents I know.

LEADER: When you have completed the Bible Study, move on to the Caring Time (page 35).

8. In what ways do you discipline your children? What do you hope to accomplish by these methods of discipline?

9. When it comes to disciplining your children, do you feel in control of the situation? Rate yourself on the scale below:

1	2	3	4	5	6	7	8	9	10
I'm about to "crash and burn"			I'm slipping and sliding but heading in the right direction					I'm in total control	

COMMENT

Didn't you love it when you had friends over to your house, or when your parents had visitors? Part of the excitement was that it was different than your normal routine. But the best part was that most of our parents' rules and discipline came to a screeching halt. We could skip our chores, be excused from practicing our musical instrument, and stay up later than usual.

While it was good to get a break once in a while (and not to live constantly with an inflexible regimen), total freedom wasn't what we really wanted. Discipline not only prepared us for life as adults, it also made us happier and more secure as kids.

The writer of Hebrews stresses this point in his letter. Using the everyday experience of family life, he reminds his readers that parents sometimes demonstrate their love and devotion to their children through discipline. Likewise, one of the ways God shows us how much he loves us is by disciplining us. Discipline is not the same as punishment, however. If parents aren't confused about the two, it's more likely that their children won't be confused either.

♡ CARING TIME/20 Minutes/All Together

Leader: Bring all of the foursomes back together for a time of caring. Follow the three steps below.

SHARING — Share with the person next to you one area of your relationship with your children which needs improvement.

PRAYER — **GO AHEAD AND ASK!** Asking God for something is an important type of prayer. This can be a prayer for yourself or for someone else. Use the list below to help you decide what to pray about.

Ourselves, such as:
- ☐ families
- ☐ personal growth
- ☐ health
- ☐ money
- ☐ crisis
- ☐ self-control

Our small group, including:
- ☐ building community
- ☐ finding new members
- ☐ choosing a mission or task
- ☐ deciding what to study next

Our families:
- ☐ improving communication
- ☐ getting along
- ☐ making a decision
- ☐ raising children
- ☐ building trust
- ☐ loving each other

Our church, such as:
- ☐ leadership
- ☐ helping the less fortunate
- ☐ youth and children
- ☐ building program
- ☐ evangelism
- ☐ worship services
- ☐ finances
- ☐ new members

The government, including:
- ☐ city government
- ☐ state government
- ☐ particular legislation
- ☐ county government
- ☐ federal government
- ☐ community leaders

Those without Christ:
- ☐ Christless friends
- ☐ countries and regions without churches
- ☐ people who feel unloved

Our society, including:
- ☐ moral problems
- ☐ poverty
- ☐ inflation
- ☐ violence
- ☐ crime
- ☐ youth
- ☐ purposelessness
- ☐ unemployment

Our world:
- ☐ war
- ☐ prejudice
- ☐ economic issues
- ☐ famine
- ☐ oppression
- ☐ environmental problems

ACTION

What area of your relationship with your children needs improvement? What can you do to improve this? In what practical ways can Scriptural teachings be applied to improve your relationship with your children?

What are you going to do at the close of this course to celebrate? Now's the time to start planning.

SESSION 5
Parents in Pain

PURPOSE: To learn that communication is the key to resolve family conflict.

AGENDA: 🍵 Gathering 📖 Bible Study ♡ Caring Time

OPEN

🍵 GATHERING/10 Minutes/All Together

Leader: Read the instructions for Step One and go first. Then read the Introduction and explain the Bible Study choices.

Step One: FAMILY CONNECTIONS. Talking about your family with your small group is a good way for everyone in the group to understand each other. In the space below, draw a circle for each one of your family members, and write their name inside it. Next, draw a solid line between people in your family who care about each other. Draw a dotted line between family members who are ambivalent about each other. Draw a jagged line between family members who do not get along.

INTRODUCTION

Step Two: PARENTS IN PAIN. While parenting children of any age has its challenges, the challenges of parenting teenagers seem to multiply one hundred times over! With all of the physical changes and those mischievous hormones pulsing through their bodies, adolescent children are often more than we can handle. Besides the hormonal changes, adolescence is a time of struggling with identity, as psychoanalyst Erik Erickson stated. At this time, a child wants to discover who he or she is. The adolescent tests boundaries and tries out new behaviors in search of that identity. The challenge of parenting at this time is to keep firm boundaries in line, while at the same time encouraging independence and self-exploration. Conflict is a common experience in families with children of this age.

Even the most loving families experience friction when people live under the same roof. Some of this conflict (like what we talked about in our opening session) is usually just light banter and produces little hostility or pain. The strains of keeping a marriage healthy, raising children, and making ends meet combine to make a fertile soil for family conflict. Who's going to feed the baby at 3 AM? Who tracked mud all over the newly-cleaned kitchen floor? Who's been squeezing the toothpaste tube in the middle? Who splurged on new spring clothes and wiped out the family budget?

But some of the conflict cuts to the heart of who we are. Children feel misunderstood or not taken seriously. Parents feel as if they aren't being respected, or they feel uncertain to what to do next. If such conflict is not dealt with in a redemptive manner, family conflict can cause deep pain well into the children's adulthood.

Family conflict does not have to blow a family apart. Through loving patience and understanding, conflict can actually draw a family together. Communication is the key. Solutions to conflict can usually be found when members are able to freely talk and listen without being devastated. Sometimes, however, outside help is needed, and a family should not be ashamed to call on a minister or professional counselor when necessary.

LEADER: Choose the Option One Bible Study (page 39) or the Option Two Study (page 42).

In the following Option One Study (from Luke's Gospel), we will see a father's pain and a son's rebellion turn into a tearful reunion. And in the Option Two Study (from Paul's second letter to the Corinthians), we will see how Paul dealt with his "parental pain" with the church. Remember, the purpose of the Bible Study is to talk about the pain in your life as a parent.

OPTION 1

 BIBLE STUDY/30 Minutes/Groups of 4

Leader: Help the group decide on Option One or Option Two for their Bible Study. Remember to divide into groups of four if there are more than seven. Ask one person in each group to be the Convener. Remind the Convener to move the group along so the Bible Study can be completed in 30 minutes.

Gospel Study/Fracas in the Family
Luke 15:11–32

STUDY

Read Luke 15:11–32 and discuss your responses to the following questions with your group. This is one of the most famous of Jesus' parables, and was told in response to the outrage of the Pharisees (religious leaders of the time) over Jesus' association with people who were "sinners."

¹¹ Jesus continued: "There was a man who had two sons. ¹² The younger one said to his father, 'Father, give me my share of the estate.' So he divided his property between them.

¹³ "Not long after that, the younger son got together all he had, set off for a distant country and there squandered his wealth in wild living. ¹⁴ After he had spent everything, there was a severe famine in that whole country, and he began to be in need. ¹⁵ So he went and hired himself out to a citizen of that country, who sent him to his fields to feed pigs. ¹⁶ He longed to fill his stomach with the pods that the pigs were eating, but no one gave him anything.

¹⁷ "When he came to his senses, he said, 'How many of my father's hired men have food to spare, and here I am starving to death! ¹⁸ I will set out and go back to my father and say to him: Father, I have sinned against heaven and against you. ¹⁹ I am no longer worthy to be called your son; make me like one of your hired men.' ²⁰ So he got up and went to his father.

"But while he was still a long way off, his father saw him and was filled with compassion for him; he ran to his son, threw his arms around him and kissed him.

²¹ "The son said to him, 'Father, I have sinned against heaven and against you. I am no longer worthy to be called your son.'

²² "But the father said to his servants, 'Quick! Bring the best robe and put it on him. Put a ring on his finger and sandals on his feet. ²³ Bring the fattened calf and kill it. Let's have a feast and celebrate. ²⁴ For this son of mine was dead and is alive again; he was lost and is found.' So they began to celebrate.

²⁵ "Meanwhile, the older son was in the field. When he came near the house, he heard music and dancing. ²⁶ So he called one of the servants and

asked him what was going on. ²⁷ *'Your brother has come,' he replied, 'and your father has killed the fattened calf because he has him back safe and sound.'*
²⁸ *"The older brother became angry and refused to go in. So his father went out and pleaded with him.* ²⁹ *But he answered his father, 'Look! All these years I've been slaving for you and never disobeyed your orders. Yet you never gave me even a young goat so I could celebrate with my friends.* ³⁰ *But when this son of yours who has squandered your property with prostitutes comes home, you kill the fattened calf for him!'*
³¹ *" 'My son,' the father said, 'you are always with me, and everything I have is yours.* ³² *But we had to celebrate and be glad, because this brother of yours was dead and is alive again; he was lost and is found.' "*

Luke 15:11–32, NIV

> "The problems of America are the family problems multiplied a million-fold."
> —Dwight D. Eisenhower

1. If you were to project yourself into this story, which character would you identify with? Why?
   - ❐ the younger son—I've squandered my allowance (and even sown a few wild oats).
   - ❐ the older son—I've resented younger siblings who had privileges I didn't.
   - ❐ the waiting father—My kids keep me up.
   - ❐ the narrator—I'm a spectator watching what God is doing in the lives of others.
   - ❐ the younger son—I've experienced grace despite my actions.
   - ❐ the older son—I've felt that I've had to be good.
   - ❐ the pigs—I've been with prodigals who hit bottom.

2. Why did the father let the son leave so easily?
   - ❐ He had no control over his younger son.
   - ❐ His son would have left no matter what he did.
   - ❐ He knew his son would have to learn in "the School of Hard Knocks."
   - ❐ He didn't care what his younger son did.

3. What is your attitude toward the suffering of the younger son?
   - ❐ He deserved all that happened to him.
   - ❐ It's too bad he had to learn so much the hard way.
   - ❐ Everyone goes through a similar experience.
   - ❐ He was a fool; his suffering was inevitable.

4. When the younger son returned home, what would have been your attitude (as his parent)?
   - ❏ Good to see you—but you're grounded!
   - ❏ You have disgraced the family.
   - ❏ Where's the money?
   - ❏ I don't approve of your actions, but you're still my son.
   - ❏ Welcome home, son—I love you!

5. When did you leave home for the first time? What were some of the circumstances surrounding your departure? Where did you go when you left your parents' home? How did you feel at that time?

6. Which of the patterns for resolving family conflict in this story are typical of you and/or family members?
   - ❏ insist on doing things my way, right or wrong
   - ❏ tow the line, give in to "father knows best"
   - ❏ lovingly let people suffer the consequences of their own decisions
   - ❏ stick to your business, avoid the conflict, and let time heal all wounds

7. Which relationship in your family generates the most conflict? Why?
   - ❏ father and son
   - ❏ father and daughter
   - ❏ mother and son
   - ❏ mother and daughter
   - ❏ brother and brother
   - ❏ sister and sister
   - ❏ sister and brother
   - ❏ husband and wife

8. What are you doing (or planning to do) differently with your children than what your parents did with you? Explain your answer.
   - ❏ nothing differently
   - ❏ a few things
   - ❏ everything differently

9. Spiritually, where are you in relationship with God the Father?
   - ❏ in a far country
   - ❏ now just coming to my senses
   - ❏ on my way home
   - ❏ home, but just barely
   - ❏ at home, enjoying a good relationship
   - ❏ other: _____

LEADER: When you have completed the Bible Study, move on to the Caring Time (page 45).

10. How does your relationship to God the Father affect the pain you experience as a parent?
   - ❏ It helps me to know that God experiences the same pain in relation to us.
   - ❏ It helps to know God will give me the strength I need.
   - ❏ It helps to know my children are ultimately in God's hands.
   - ❏ It does not affect my pain one way or another.

OPTION 2

Epistle Study/Painful Times
2 Corinthians 1:23–2:4

STUDY

Read 2 Corinthians 1:23–2:4 and discuss your responses to the following questions with your group. Paul had a painful and troubled relationship with the church at Corinth, and this relationship seems to have generated more letters than Paul wrote to any other church. Central sources of those conflicts were their divisions as a church and their questioning of his authority. This passage (from one of his letters) expresses his feelings about those conflicts.

²³ I call God as my witness that it was in order to spare you that I did not return to Corinth. ²⁴ Not that we lord it over your faith, but we work with you for your joy, because it is by faith you stand firm. ¹ So I made up my mind that I would not make another painful visit to you. ² For if I grieve you, who is left to make me glad but you whom I have grieved? ³ I wrote as I did so that when I came I should not be distressed by those who ought to make me rejoice. I had confidence in all of you, that you would all share my joy. ⁴ For I wrote you out of great distress and anguish of heart and with many tears, not to grieve you but to let you know the depth of my love for you.

2 Corinthians 1:23–2:4, NIV

1. Which word would you use to describe Paul's feelings as he wrote this passage?
   - ❏ angry
   - ❏ hurt
   - ❏ sad
   - ❏ defensive
   - ❏ loving
   - ❏ grief-stricken

2. If you had to compare your household to a television show, which one of the following would best describe it? Why?
   - ❏ the Cleavers
   - ❏ the Huxtables
   - ❏ the Keatons (*Family Ties*)
   - ❏ the Waltons
   - ❏ the Simpsons
   - ❏ the Connors (*Roseanne*)
   - ❏ the Nelsons
   - ❏ the Brady Bunch

3. What causes most parents the greatest pain?
   - ❏ their overwhelming responsibilities
   - ❏ their inability to make decisions
   - ❏ their lack of self-confidence
   - ❏ disrespectful children
   - ❏ irresponsible children
   - ❏ disobedient children
   - ❏ other: _____

4. What was the standard "line" or "command" from your parents every time you left home? Is this old command so ingrained in you that you now find yourself occasionally saying the same thing to your children?
   - ❏ "Don't get into trouble."
   - ❏ "Don't embarrass the family."
   - ❏ "If you're late, you're grounded."
   - ❏ "Don't hang around with so-and-so."
   - ❏ "Remember, you're not like the other kids."
   - ❏ other: _____

5. How did your parents exercise authority over you in your childhood years?
   - ❏ I knew who was in charge of any situation—they were.
   - ❏ They loved and disciplined me in fair ways.
   - ❏ Their love and discipline provided me with a lot of freedom.
   - ❏ They controlled every situation (and me).
   - ❏ There was more discipline than love.
   - ❏ I always knew that they were my parents, but they allowed me to make my own decisions.
   - ❏ other: _____

> *"Loving relationships are a family's best protection against the challenges of the world."*
> —Bernie Wiebe

6. How do you (plan to) exercise authority over your children?
- ☐ let them know that I am in charge
- ☐ love and discipline them in fair ways
- ☐ love and discipline them with a lot of freedom
- ☐ control them and every situation
- ☐ strict discipline, less love
- ☐ let them know that I am their parent, but allow them to make their own decisions
- ☐ other: _____

7. How should discipline change when a child enters the teenage years?
- ☐ Less physical discipline should be used, and more restriction and social discipline.
- ☐ More freedom to choose should be allowed.
- ☐ Parents should talk more about the reasons behind rules and discipline.
- ☐ Parents need to help children learn self-discipline.
- ☐ Parents have to be even tougher.
- ☐ Discipline should not change when children reach this age.
- ☐ other: _____

8. When have you experienced what Paul discussed here (vv. 2–4)—what was meant as an expression of love for his "children" caused them grief? What did you do to clarify your intent and find healing in the relationship?

9. How prepared were/are you for the troublesome times with your children?
- ☐ totally unprepared
- ☐ partially prepared
- ☐ prepared as I can be
- ☐ totally prepared
- ☐ I don't want to talk about it
- ☐ other: _____

LEADER: When you have completed the Bible Study, move on to the Caring Time (below).

10. What can you do to be more prepared for those troubling times?
☐ read a book on parenting
☐ take a course on parenting
☐ talk with other parents
☐ talk with my parents
☐ No need to do anything more—God will take care of us.
☐ continue to provide a loving and structured life for them
☐ Everything is fine—I am fully prepared.
☐ pray more
☐ other: _____

COMMENT

Rearing children in today's society is a monumental task. Many parents are completely overwhelmed by the thought of their children becoming teenagers. Don't despair! Others (probably even in your group) have the same concerns. No one is a perfect parent, and we can learn from each other. Continue to pray for God's guidance and share your concerns with others.

♡ CARING TIME/20 Minutes/All Together
Leader: Bring all of the foursomes back together for a time of caring. Follow the steps below.

SELF-CARE

INDULGE YOURSELF! Take care of yourself! Here is a chance for you to choose a way you are going to be good to yourself. Here's how it works: Take a look at the list below (and on page 46) and choose one thing that you are going to do for yourself before your next meeting. Take turns telling the group what you have chosen. At your next meeting, the group will ask you if you took care of yourself the way you planned.

"Before our next meeting, I'm going to take care of myself by...":

☐ getting a massage
☐ organizing my closet/desk/bookshelves
☐ buying a new outfit of clothes
☐ splurging on a gourmet dinner
☐ taking a personal retreat
☐ praying for ____ minutes each day
☐ walking or running ____ miles
☐ sitting at poolside and enjoying the sun
☐ grabbing a friend and doing something I've always wanted to do

- ☐ taking a trip
- ☐ buying fresh-cut flowers
- ☐ having a slumber party
- ☐ getting a facial/manicure/pedicure
- ☐ making my favorite dessert
- ☐ buying the gadget I've wanted
- ☐ cutting out TV/junk food/tobacco/alcohol

SHARING   In light of our Bible Study on family conflicts, briefly share with the group either a conflict you are presently in or a conflict of which you are aware. For example, "Please pray for me and my daughter," or "Please pray for my spouse and her/his father."

PRAYER   Remembering the requests which were just shared, close with a prayer time. The Leader can start a conversational prayer (short phrases and sentences), with group members following. After an appropriate amount of time, the Leader can close the time of prayer by praying for any requests not already mentioned.

ACTION   On an index card, write your first name and a prayer request you have about raising your children. Randomly distribute the cards, and ask everyone to pray for the person on their card throughout the next week.

SESSION 6
Parental Expectations

PURPOSE: To discover the stressful impact of expectations on family life.

AGENDA: ☕ Gathering 📖 Bible Study ♡ Caring Time

OPEN

☕ **GATHERING/10 Minutes/All Together**

Leader: Continue to be sensitive to all who share. By this time, group members should feel comfortable enough with each other to share at a deeper level. Read the instructions for Step One and go first. Then read the Introduction and explain the choices for Bible Study.

Step One: THE GREAT AMERICAN BLUSH AWARDS. Imagine your group is in charge of giving an award for the most embarrassing thing a child has done to his or her parents. Instead of an "Emmy" we can call it a "Ruddy." Find out who in your group has had a child do the following. Then vote on which is the most embarrassing. Give that person (or persons) the "Ruddy"!

❐ had a child share an embarrassing family incident during the children's sermon
❐ had a child report a less-than-flattering remark you made about someone else
❐ had an older child dress oddly when company came over
❐ when a single parent, had a child propose to your date for you
❐ had a child bring out embarrassing hygiene products for company
❐ had a child publicly contradict your "little white lie"
❐ had a little girl lifting her dress during a public function
❐ had a child repeat a "four-letter-word" with others asking where he or she learned it
❐ had a little child shout during a quiet moment of worship, "I have to go potty!"
❐ other: _____

INTRODUCTION

Step Two: PARENTAL EXPECTATIONS. Excessive stress is epidemic in our society, and families are not immune to it. Frazzled parents escape the wear-and-tear of the workplace only to come home to the stressful demands of the family. The innocence of childhood is often interrupted by the gut-wrenching sound of parents fighting. And the balance in the checkbook never seems to move very far from zero. But while every family experiences some stress, the home can often be a sanctuary from stress. Studies have shown that many men and women believe their family life counterbalances job stress.

Sometimes stress is caused by unrealistic expectations. Everyone dreams about their ideal life. And occasionally, we all play the "if only ..." game. Parents are no different. Often, in wanting the best for their children, the parents' expectations may get in the way of what the child really wants. This is often demonstrated at athletic events for kids, when their overzealous parents become the expert coach or referee.

It's natural for parents to want the best for their kids. And it's natural for parents to expect certain things from their children. But stress and tension mount when parental expectations take over and differ with their children's wishes (and maybe even God's plans).

LEADER: Choose the Option One Study (below) or the Option Two Study (page 51).

In the Option One Study, this is precisely what happened with the mother of James and John. We will study how Jesus handled this situation in Matthew's Gospel. In the Option Two Study (from Paul's letter to the Colossians), we will discover God's expectations for us. Remember, in this session, the issue is your life as a parent. Use the Scripture passages to walk into your story with your group.

OPTION 1

 BIBLE STUDY/30 Minutes/Groups of 4

Leader: Help the group choose an Option for study. Divide into groups of four for discussion. Remind the Convener for each foursome to move the group along so the Bible Study can be completed in the time allotted. Ask everyone to return together for the Caring Time for the final 20 minutes.

Gospel Study/A Mother's Request
Matthew 20:20–28

STUDY

Read Matthew 20:20–28 and discuss your responses to the following questions with your group. This incident occurred late in Jesus' earthly ministry, and details a "jockeying for position" at a time when the disciples expected Jesus' kingdom to come soon.

²⁰ Then the mother of Zebedee's sons came to Jesus with her sons and, kneeling down, asked a favor of him.

²¹ "What is it you want?" he asked.

She said, "Grant that one of these two sons of mine may sit at your right and the other at your left in your kingdom."

²² "You don't know what you are asking," Jesus said to them. "Can you drink the cup I am going to drink?"

"We can," they answered.

²³ Jesus said to them, "You will indeed drink from my cup, but to sit at my right or left is not for me to grant. These places belong to those for whom they have been prepared by my Father."

²⁴ When the ten heard about this, they were indignant with the two brothers. ²⁵ Jesus called them together and said, "You know that the rulers of the Gentiles lord it over them, and their high officials exercise authority over them. ²⁶ Not so with you. Instead, whoever wants to become great among you must be your servant, ²⁷ and whoever wants to be first must be your slave— ²⁸ just as the Son of Man did not come to be served, but to serve, and to give his life as a ransom for many."

Matthew 20:20–28, NIV

1. Who are you embarrassed for in this story?
   - ❐ Jesus—for having to refuse the mother's request
   - ❐ the mother of the two sons
   - ❐ the two sons—James and John

2. Why do you think the mother did this?
   - ❐ Her two sons put her up to this.
   - ❐ She was just acting like a mother.
   - ❐ She wanted the best for her sons.
   - ❐ She didn't realize what she was asking.

3. What was the mother really asking for?
   - ❐ special recognition for her sons
   - ❐ a closer relationship with Jesus
   - ❐ her own sense of satisfaction
   - ❐ power and position
   - ❐ spiritual security

"Those who dwell continually upon their expectations are apt to become oblivious to the requirements of their actual situation."
—Charles Sanders Pierce

4. When Jesus told the mother, "You don't know what you are asking," what did he mean?
   - ❏ Ma'am, you're embarrassing your sons.
   - ❏ You've got to be kidding.
   - ❏ Your sons don't deserve that honor.
   - ❏ Sorry—it's not my decision to make.

5. What is the closest your mother (or father) came to embarrassing you in public?
   - ❏ insisting that you "perform" for the relatives
   - ❏ showing your baby pictures to your girlfriend/boyfriend
   - ❏ coming to a school event and clapping or cheering too loudly
   - ❏ telling a secret family story to your high school friends
   - ❏ crying at your wedding
   - ❏ other: _____

6. What did your parents want you to be when you grew up? What did you want to be?

7. Which of the following comes closest to the truth concerning your parent's expectations of you?
   - ❏ My parents expected very little, causing me to doubt my ability.
   - ❏ My parents expected perfection, causing me to be dissatisfied with all I did.
   - ❏ My parent's expectations were high enough to challenge me, and low enough to be reachable.
   - ❏ My parents helped me to develop my own set of expectations.

8. Are you living up to your parents' expectations?
   - ❏ You can't be serious!
   - ❏ I've given up trying.
   - ❏ I'm trying.
   - ❏ Yes.
   - ❏ My parents didn't lay any expectations on me.

9. As you read what Jesus told this mother, what does it imply for you about your expectations for your children?
   - ☐ I need to stop being a "stage mother."
   - ☐ I need to stop speaking on behalf of my children and let them speak on their own behalf.
   - ☐ I need to help my children focus less on self-glory and more on how they can serve.
   - ☐ Before I encourage my children to reach for something, I should be sure I know the cost.
   - ☐ other: _____

LEADER: When you have completed the Bible Study, move on to the Caring Time (page 54).

10. What would you like to pass on to your kids?
    - ☐ nothing in particular—They need to develop on their own.
    - ☐ a sense of right and wrong
    - ☐ a deep faith
    - ☐ loyalty to the family
    - ☐ unconditional acceptance
    - ☐ significant wealth
    - ☐ other: _____

11. How will you pass these things on to your kids?

OPTION 2

Epistle Study/God's Expectations
Colossians 3:1–17

STUDY

Read Colossians 3:1–17 and discuss your responses to the following questions with your group. This letter was written to the church at Colossae, which was a Greek city. At that time, Greeks did not have high moral expectations of people, especially with respect to sexual morality. In this passage, Paul sets some higher expectations for them.

3 *Since, then, you have been raised with Christ, set your hearts on things above, where Christ is seated at the right hand of God. ² Set your minds on things above, not on earthly things. ³ For you died, and your life is now hidden with Christ in God. ⁴ When Christ, who is your life, appears, then you also will appear with him in glory.*

⁵ Put to death, therefore, whatever belongs to your earthly nature: sexual immorality, impurity, lust, evil desires and greed, which is idolatry. ⁶ Because of these, the wrath of God is coming. ⁷ You used to walk in these ways, in the life you once lived. ⁸ But now you must rid yourselves of all such things as these: anger, rage, malice, slander, and filthy language from your lips. ⁹ Do not lie to each other, since you have taken off your old self with its practices ¹⁰ and have put on the new self, which is being renewed in knowledge in the image of its Creator. ¹¹ Here there is no Greek or Jew, circumcised or uncircumcised, barbarian, Scythian, slave or free, but Christ is all, and is in all.

¹² Therefore, as God's chosen people, holy and dearly loved, clothe yourselves with compassion, kindness, humility, gentleness and patience. ¹³ Bear with each other and forgive whatever grievances you may have against one another. Forgive as the Lord forgave you. ¹⁴ And over all these virtues put on love, which binds them all together in perfect unity.

¹⁵ Let the peace of Christ rule in your hearts, since as members of one body you were called to peace. And be thankful. ¹⁶ Let the word of Christ dwell in you richly as you teach and admonish one another with all wisdom, and as you sing psalms, hymns and spiritual songs with gratitude in your hearts to God. ¹⁷ And whatever you do, whether in word or deed, do it all in the name of the Lord Jesus, giving thanks to God the Father through him.

Colossians 3:1–17, NIV

1. If you heard Paul's letter for the first time, what would you think? (Be honest.)
   - ❐ Paul, it sounds a bit "pie in the sky"
   - ❐ yeah, sure... like tomorrow
   - ❐ I don't remember seeing all of those things in your life, Paul.
   - ❐ Wow—I guess I have a lot of work to do.
   - ❐ Wow—I guess God and I have a lot of work to do.
   - ❐ There's no use trying to live up to these expectations.

2. Growing up, what expectations did your parents have for you?

3. How did their expectations differ from your expectations for yourself?
   - ❐ Their expectations were much higher (or harder) than mine.
   - ❐ Their expectations were much lower (or easier) than mine.
   - ❐ We shared similar expectations.
   - ❐ My parents never had expectations for me.
   - ❐ It didn't matter to me what they expected.

> "God does not expect us to imitate Jesus Christ. He expects us to allow the life of Jesus to be manifested."
> —Oswald Chambers

4. If you were to tack a list of expectations on your children's wall (as Paul lists in this passage) what would their reaction be?
   - ❏ "Can I apply for adoption?"
   - ❏ "I will do these things when I see you doing them!"
   - ❏ "What does all of this mean?"
   - ❏ "Finally! Some clear expectations!"
   - ❏ "This should make it easier to live around here!"
   - ❏ nothing different—This is what has been expected of them all along.

5. Using one word or a short phrase, what are your expectations of your children in each of these areas:
   morally _____
   relationally _____
   in relation to God _____
   educationally _____
   in achievements _____
   in behavior towards me _____

6. How do your expectations for your children mesh with God's expectations?
   - ❏ They are one and the same.
   - ❏ There is significant overlap.
   - ❏ There are some similarities.
   - ❏ They are vastly different.

7. How can you help your children accept or meet God's expectations?

8. Answer true (T) or false (F) to the following statements and discuss your responses with the group:
   ___ How well a family handles stress is largely determined by its emotional health.
   ___ Any stressful situation can be met if the family has adequate financial resources.
   ___ Whether or not a situation is really stressful depends a great deal on the definition a family gives it.
   ___ Open grieving at the death of a family member should be encouraged as a way of alleviating stress from loss.
   ___ If an individual is under excessive stress, then his/her family will also be under excessive stress.
   ___ Stress can actually serve to strengthen a family.
   ___ Unrealistic expectations will most likely cause stress in a family.

LEADER: When you have completed the Bible Study, move on to the Caring Time (page 54).

COMMENT

Most parents have expectations for their children, whether or not the parents express them. One of the questions parents need to ask themselves is whether their expectations coincide or conflict with God's expectations.

As Christians, we are to pattern our lives on God's ways—not the ways of the world. Every day we need to turn away from attitudes and actions which reflect our old way of life. In verses 5–9, Paul lists sins that God expects us to give up in our lives. Although this isn't an easy command to follow, God's Spirit is ready and able to help us make tough choices.

But that is not all. Paul continues (in vv. 12–17) to outline God's expectations for us about the way we ought to live. Again, the Spirit who is in us can help us to fulfill these expectations. Periodically, we need to check and see if our expectations are in line with God's expectations. If they aren't, stress and strain are bound to exist—complicating our lives even further.

CARING TIME/20 Minutes/All Together

Leader: Bring all of the foursomes back together for a time of caring. Follow the steps below.

AFFIRMATION

YOU REMIND ME OF ... This is a heart-warmer from Serendipity's *Ice-Breakers and Heart-Warmers*. Write your name on a slip of paper and put it in a hat. Let everyone in the group select a name from the hat, but don't tell anyone whose name you have drawn. Choose a national park that best describes the person you have selected. When everyone is finished, read out loud the national park you chose and see if the group can guess who you are describing.

- ❏ **Grand Canyon National Park:** What an impressive vista! You have character that has taken years of patient effort and constant attention.

- ❏ **Golden Gate National Park:** You bring people together and bridge the gap in a beautiful, stunning way.

- ❏ **Sequoia National Park:** Your growth is so impressive that you reach into the skies and provide shade and security for many different creatures.

- **Yosemite National Park:** You are the most popular choice for an exciting and adventurous experience!

- **Mammoth Cave National Park:** With hundreds of miles of underground passageways, you epitomize depth, mystery, and hidden treasures.

- **Statue of Liberty National Monument:** You are a living symbol to those around you of freedom, hope, and a new life.

- **Mount Rushmore:** You are an enduring testimony to leadership, character, and integrity.

- **Yellowstone National Park:** With your hot springs and geysers, you are a source of warmth for those who get close to you.

- **Mount Rainier National Park:** You keep people looking up, and your high standards can be seen from a great distance.

- **The Alamo:** You remind everyone who sees you of courage, tenacity, and determination.

SHARING

Ask each group member to finish the following sentence:

"The areas where I need to change my expectations of my children are ..."

PRAYER

Ask your group to pray for these expectations which need to be changed. If someone is uncomfortable praying aloud, encourage them to pray silently. When they conclude their prayer, ask them to say "Amen," so the next person will know to continue.

ACTION

Write down the changes you need to make and put the paper in your wallet, money clip, or purse. In this way, you will come across it frequently, and it will remind you of what you need to work on. Each time you come across it, pray for God's strength and direction to make this change.

SESSION 7
Family of God

PURPOSE: To understand that the Christian church is the family of God, and a model for all families.

AGENDA: Gathering | Bible Study | Caring Time

OPEN

GATHERING/10 Minutes/All Together

Leader: This is the final session together. You may want to have your Caring Time first. If not, be sure to allow a full 25 minutes at the end of the session. Read the instructions for Step One and set the pace by going first. Then read the Introduction and move on to the Bible Study.

Step One: SELF-AFFIRMATION. Complete the following sentences and take turns telling the group about yourself:

- ❒ **I have** ... (two things you like about your appearance)
- ❒ **I take care of myself by** ... (one thing you do that is healthy)
- ❒ **At work, I am very good at** ... (two things you excel at on the job)
- ❒ **I contribute to a caring relationship by** ... (one thing you do to maintain a good friendship)

When each person is finished sharing their answers about themselves, the rest of the group should stand up and give them a standing ovation.

INTRODUCTION

Step Two: FAMILY OF GOD. The Bible uses the analogy of the family (specifically the family of God) to describe the relationship of Christians to God, and of Christians to each other. Jesus taught that if we did God's will, we were his "brothers and sisters." Christians are often described in Scripture as the "children of God" and the "sons [daughters] of God." In their New Testament writings, the apostles Paul, James, and John each address their fellow Christians as brothers and sisters.

The representation of the Christian church as the family of God is intentional. The family has been an enduring part of virtually every civilization. The family is the showcase for parental love. The family is the cocoon within which children grow and mature. The family provides an environment where love can germinate and flourish.

LEADER: Choose the Option One Study (below) or the Option Two Study (page 60).

In the Option One Study (from Mark's Gospel), Jesus defines the members of the family of God. And in the Option Two Study (from the letter to the Ephesians), Paul describes how God has created his family out of diverse people, from those who were once enemies. In both passages, the important point is that we become members of God's family through Jesus Christ; specifically (as Paul shows) as a result of Christ's death on the cross.

OPTION 1

 BIBLE STUDY/25 Minutes/Groups of 4

Leader: For this final session, again divide into groups of four (if there are more than seven in your group). Help the groups choose their Bible Study. Remind the Conveners to end their Bible Study time five minutes earlier than usual to allow ample time for your final Caring Time—deciding what the group will do next.

Gospel Study/All in the Family
Mark 3:20–21, 31–35

STUDY

Read Mark 3:20–21, 31–35 and discuss your responses to the following questions with your group. The Gospel of Mark presents Jesus as being under a lot of pressure from the crowd once they discovered he could heal them. Their demands made it so difficult for him to have time to himself that Jesus' mother and siblings felt the need to rescue him.

²⁰ Then Jesus entered a house, and again a crowd gathered, so that he and his disciples were not even able to eat. ²¹ When his family heard about this, they went to take charge of him, for they said, "He is out of his mind."

³¹ Then Jesus' mother and brothers arrived. Standing outside, they sent someone in to call him. ³² A crowd was sitting around him, and they told him, "Your mother and brothers are outside looking for you."
³³ "Who are my mother and my brothers?" he asked.
³⁴ Then he looked at those seated in a circle around him and said, "Here are my mother and my brothers! ³⁵ Whoever does God's will is my brother and sister and mother."

Mark 3:20–21, 31–35, NIV

1. Imagine you were a reporter for *The Galilean Gazette* and had been assigned to cover this story. Which headline would you use?
   - ❏ "New Rabbi Rumored to be Unstable"
   - ❏ "Rescue Operation Rebuffed"
   - ❏ "Prophet Spews Anti-Family Rhetoric"
   - ❏ " 'We Can be Family,' Announces Prophet"
   - ❏ " 'Do God's Will!' Declares Famous Healer"

2. Why did Jesus' family want to "take charge of him"?
   - ❏ They feared that he would overwork himself.
   - ❏ They thought he had "delusions of grandeur."
   - ❏ He was embarrassing his family.
   - ❏ They wanted to teach him proper behavior.

3. What would you have done if you had been a member of Jesus' family?
   - ❏ I'd have gone into the house and confronted him.
   - ❏ I'd have spoken to Jesus privately.
   - ❏ I'd have been too embarrassed to do anything.
   - ❏ I'd have ordered him to go home and be quiet.
   - ❏ Nothing—I wouldn't have wanted to make a scene.

4. In referring to the crowd, why did Jesus answer by saying, "Here are my mother and my brothers"?
   - ❏ He believed he belonged to the family of all humanity.
   - ❏ He was redefining the "family of God."
   - ❏ He placed more importance on his spiritual family than on his natural family.
   - ❏ He was teaching the crowd that they could belong to the family of God.

5. As a kid, what crazy stunt did you pull which embarrassed your family (or would have embarrassed them if they had known about it)?

6. How do you feel about the family you have (either the family you grew up in, or the one you are raising now)?
   - ❏ I love each and every one of them.
   - ❏ I don't know how I kept my sanity, but I did.
   - ❏ Ours was/is a household of pain.
   - ❏ Our family life was/is full of tension.
   - ❏ I (my kids) grew up feeling secure in my (their) parents' love
   - ❏ I grew up feeling insecure, and searched for others to accept me
   - ❏ other: _____

"No family, whether it has ten children or two, should function as a closed, isolated entity."
—Peter Uhlenberg

7. According to these verses, what is necessary for you to become a member of the family of God?
   - ☐ You must turn your back on your natural family.
   - ☐ You must know and follow the will of God.
   - ☐ You must believe that Jesus is the Son of God.
   - ☐ You must be adopted by Jesus.

8. Which two of the following statements describe your relationship with the family of God?
   - ☐ I have been in the family for quite a while.
   - ☐ I consider myself to be a "black sheep" in the family.
   - ☐ I'm really on the outside looking in.
   - ☐ I'm just a baby in the family.
   - ☐ I generally don't get along with other family members.
   - ☐ I know the family history "inside and out."
   - ☐ I love all my relatives.
   - ☐ I love most of my relatives.
   - ☐ I've got a lot to learn about this family.
   - ☐ I want to spend more time with my Father.

LEADER: When you have completed the Bible Study, move on to the Caring Time (page 62).

9. What role can parents take in helping their children to be part of the larger family of God?
   - ☐ They should not to try to protect children from the challenges God sets before them.
   - ☐ They should always affirm people of other cultures and races as part of the family.
   - ☐ They should realize that children at some point need to separate from the control of earthly parents, but not from our heavenly Parent.
   - ☐ They should be faithful in teaching them God's will.
   - ☐ other: _____

COMMENT

This is the first time we hear about Jesus' family. And they make quite an entrance! Jesus' family is concerned about him. What was causing his strange behavior? They aren't sure what is happening to him. Maybe he isn't able to care for himself. In addition, his message of God's kingdom was causing quite a stir everywhere. It was quite understandable that the opposition Jesus faced from the religious leaders concerned his family as well.

The family travelled about thirty miles from Nazareth to Capernaum. Their plan was set: they would take him back home with them—forcibly if they had to. After hearing Jesus, his family decides that he really must be out of his mind. It probably was some sort of ecstatic, religiously-induced mental illness. Jesus is surrounded by a crowd, so they don't want to confront him publicly. They send someone in to ask him to come out. Told that his family is outside, Jesus asks a rhetorical question, but nonetheless it causes more concern for the family.

Jesus provides a new definition of family. His family is not one of heredity, but of the Spirit of God. Neither the crowds nor his family understand what he is saying. However, his family will eventually move from doubt to faith.

OPTION 2

Epistle Study/Forever Family
Ephesians 2:11–22

STUDY

Read Ephesians 2:11–22 and discuss your responses to the following questions with your group. Paul, whose primary ministry was to bring Gentiles (non-Jews) to Christ, here affirms how they have become full members of God's family.

¹¹ Therefore, remember that formerly you who are Gentiles by birth and called "uncircumcised" by those who call themselves "the circumcision" (that done in the body by the hands of men)—¹² remember that at that time you were separate from Christ, excluded from citizenship in Israel and foreigners to the covenants of the promise, without hope and without God in the world. ¹³ But now in Christ Jesus you who once were far away have been brought near through the blood of Christ.

¹⁴ For he himself is our peace, who has made the two one and has destroyed the barrier, the dividing wall of hostility, ¹⁵ by abolishing in his flesh the law with its commandments and regulations. His purpose was to create in himself one new man out of the two, thus making peace, ¹⁶ and in this one body to reconcile both of them to God through the cross, by which he put to death their hostility. ¹⁷ He came and preached peace to you who were far away and peace to those who were near. ¹⁸ For through him we both have access to the Father by one Spirit.

¹⁹ Consequently, you are no longer foreigners and aliens, but fellow citizens with God's people and members of God's household, ²⁰ built on the foundation of the apostles and prophets, with Christ Jesus himself as the chief cornerstone. ²¹ In him the whole building is joined together and rises to become a holy temple in the Lord. ²² And in him you too are being built together to become a dwelling in which God lives by his Spirit.

Ephesians 2:11–22, NIV

1. If Paul were in front of you, what would you say to him about this passage?
   - ☐ If Christ broke down the dividing wall, how come we still have hostility?
   - ☐ Good! I need a place where I don't feel like an alien!
   - ☐ And I thought the blood of Christ just helped me to get closer to God.
   - ☐ How can God use my "brick" in his building?
   - ☐ other: _____

2. From where did your ancestors emigrate? What did their new citizenship mean to them? What does your citizenship mean to you?

3. In high school and/or college, which groups (clubs, activities, sororities, fraternities, honor societies, professional associations) were you not a part of but wished you were? How did you feel, being on the outside looking in?

4. What relationship in your life still has walls to be knocked down? How will you remove those walls?

5. As a parent, what dividing wall would you like to break down (with Christ's help), so your children can live in a better world?
   - ☐ racism
   - ☐ the generation gap
   - ☐ divisions between rich and poor
   - ☐ national hostilities that lead to war

6. How can you build a better relationship with other members of God's family:
   - ☐ in your personal family?
   - ☐ in your workplace?
   - ☐ in your home?
   - ☐ in your church?
   - ☐ in your small group?

7. What benefits do you see in being part of God's family?
   - ☐ It fills in when our natural (or legal) family is less than what it should be.
   - ☐ It gives a sense of peace.
   - ☐ We are enriched by the love of many more people.
   - ☐ I don't see much benefit.

> *"If your father and mother, your sister and brother, if the very cat and dog in the house, are not happier for your being Christian, it is a question whether you really are."*
> —James Hudson Taylor

LEADER: When you have completed the Bible Study, move on to the Caring Time (below).

8. As a parent, what role do you need to take to help your children be part of the family of God?
   ❏ helping my children to feel included and not feel like "aliens"
   ❏ helping my children to accept the peace brought by the blood of Christ
   ❏ helping my children to break down the walls of hostility between them and other groups
   ❏ helping my children to learn how to use their "bricks" as part of God's temple
   ❏ other: _____

COMMENT

Paul moves from the problem of human alienation from God (2:1–10) to the related problem of alienation between people (2:11–22). In both cases, the problem is hostility (or enmity). In both cases, Christ is the one who, through his death, brings peace—first between God and people, but then also between human enemies. The focus of this section is on the deep hostility between Jew and Gentile. Paul begins by reminding the Gentiles of their fivefold alienation from God's plan for the world (vv. 11–12). But he then goes on to describe how Jesus' death overcame it all (vv. 13–18). Jesus abolished the law which divided (people from God; Jew from Gentile); he created a new humanity; and he reconciled this new "race" to God. Paul concludes by describing through three metaphors (kingdom, family, temple) the new reality which has emerged (vv. 19–22).

♡ CARING TIME/25 Minutes/All Together

Leader: This is decision time. These four steps are designed to help you evaluate your group experience and to decide about the future.

EVALUATION

Take a few minutes to review your experience and reflect. Go around on each point and finish the sentences.

1. I have learned the following about parenting from these Bible studies:

2. As I see it, our purpose and goal as a group was to:

3. We achieved our goal(s):
   - ❏ completely
   - ❏ almost completely
   - ❏ somewhat
   - ❏ we blew it

4. The high point in this course for me has been:
   - ❏ the Scripture exercises
   - ❏ the sharing
   - ❏ discovering myself
   - ❏ belonging to a real community of love
   - ❏ finding new life and purpose for my life
   - ❏ the fun of the fellowship

5. One of the most significant things I learned was ...

6. In my opinion, our group functioned:
   - ❏ smoothly, and we grew
   - ❏ pretty well, but we didn't grow
   - ❏ it was tough, but we grew
   - ❏ it was tough, and we didn't grow

7. The thing I appreciated most about the group as a whole is ...

CONTINUATION

Do you want to continue as a group? If so, what do you need to improve? Finish the sentence ...

"If I were to suggest one thing we could work on as a group, it would be ..."

MAKE A COVENANT

A covenant is a promise made to each other in the presence of God. Its purpose is to indicate your intention to make yourselves available to one another for the fulfillment of the purposes you share in common. In a spirit of prayer, work your way through the following sentences, trying to reach an agreement on each statement pertaining to your ongoing life together. Write out your covenant like a contract, stating your purpose, goals, and the ground rules for your group. Then ask everyone to sign.

CURRICULUM

1. The purpose of our group will be ... (finish the sentence)

2. Our goals will be ...

3. We will meet for _____ weeks, after which we will decide if we wish to continue as a group.

4. We will meet from _____ to _____ and we will strive to start on time and end on time.

5. We will meet at _____ (place) or we will rotate from house to house.

6. We will agree to the following ground rules for our group (check):

   ❏ **Priority:** While you are in the course, you give the group meetings priority.

   ❏ **Participation:** Everyone participates and no one dominates.

   ❏ **Respect:** Everyone is given the right to their own opinion, and "dumb questions" are encouraged and respected.

   ❏ **Confidentiality:** Anything that is said in the meeting is never repeated outside the meeting.

   ❏ **Empty Chair:** The group stays open to new people at every meeting, as long as they understand the ground rules.

   ❏ **Support:** Permission is given to call upon each other in time of need at any time.

   ❏ **Accountability:** We agree to let the members of the group hold us accountable to the commitments which each of us make in whatever loving ways we decide upon.

If you decide to continue as a group for a few more weeks, what are you going to use for study and discipline? There are 15 other studies available at this 201 Series level. 301 Courses, designed for deeper Bible Study with Study Notes, are also available.

For more information about small group resources and possible directions, please contact your small group coordinator or SERENDIPITY at 1-800-525-9563.